Today I went to church and was Delighted!

I t's a brand new church for me and a bit of a gem. You see I've just returned from missions in Costa Rica and wasn't expecting to find such a good church, not right away. Pastor's sermon that morning centered on personal sanctification, and the need for our working out our purging and spiritual cleansing, as the Word says we're to do. Cool I thought "Wow" he's in such agreement with me, and what I've written about here.

It's an hour and twenty minute long sermon, and in no way time enough for teaching on how to do that. Not in such a brief span. It's a good thing there's this book! It's all about the nuts and bolts of doing just that, and it's what I had to learn to do. Set in the context of full-on spiritual-warfare. Spiritual warfare instantly undertaken, as I'm too stubborn and much too distressed, too alarmed by this incredible, demonic, satanic attack.

This full-on attack from Lucifer's Kingdom, a kingdom with its myriads of assailants and oh boy, just how am I to do this sanctification stuff? What is it and how can it help? "I-am-in-trouble!" Clangs through my mind as a wicked spirit shouts. *"WHAT, YOU DARE TO CONFRONT US,"* loud as a stereo cranked up high!

≈≈≈

- My True Story -

A SPIRITUAL WARFARE ENSEMBLE:

by Paul Moehring

- Unabridged Single Volume -
Two Books in-One

≈≈≈

Print Version by CreateSpace
Charleston, SC.

Printed by Create Space, an Amazon.com Company
eStore address (i.e. www.CreateSpace.com/5944093)
Create Space, Charleston SC.

Keywords: 1. Spiritual Warfare 2. Self Deliverance 3. Deliverance
4. Demonism 5. Christian Spiritual Warfare

A Spiritual Warfare Ensemble: Contending with- Demonic
Oppression, by Paul Moehring —1st edition.
Electronic Conversion and Covers by the author.
Available on Kindle and other fine devices.
Website: www.paulmoehring.org
Blog a-building: www.moehringsbooks.com

ISBN-13: 978-0692603598
ISBN-10: 069260359X

Printed in the United States of America
09 10 – 11 10

Foreword:

≋

T here is a spiritual war going on right now and you are in it! You may be keenly aware of this fact, and this book in your hand is an attempt to learn more about this battle and how to conquer Satan and the demonic spirits he unleashes. You may sense his attempts to oppress you, and keep you from fulfilling the calling God has placed on your life. Or you may just know that there's this very real, "resistance," that's hard at work trying to keep you from living a life of peace, power and purpose. You don't fully understand it but you feel it. You are tired of it and want to overcome it. If that's you then read on. This book's author has spent a good portion of his life building and operating a dental and a prosthetics lab for a hospital ships ministry, called Mercy Ships. Paul Moehring has been in the trenches of real missionary work, designing and fabricating facial and lower limb prostheses. He has enjoyed seeing lives literally changed, serving the Lord and loving people…. and Satan has fought against him the entire journey.

With this volume (two books in one), Paul gives insights into spiritual warfare, using his own experiences from demonic oppression, and unusually, complete victory over it. Paul shares his "proven weapons of warfare" that can be used to identify, expose and repel demons that have been assigned by Satan to oppress your spirit and thwart God's plan for your life. *Each chapter carries the tone of a "personal conversation" in which Paul candidly shares his particular life story. He then closes each chapter with a clear and concise overview with "thoughts to take away" from what you've read. It's a worthwhile read.* The Apostle Paul said in Philippians 1:17, "I am set for the defense of the Gospel." He knew he was "placed" on this earth to proclaim, promote and defend the Gospel of Jesus Christ. *We all are!* We are made to worship and exalt God, to glorify His Son; to walk in the power of the Holy Spirit! We are made to serve in and build up the kingdom of God. Paul Moehring and I share the knowledge that this is the warfare. That when we chose to accept Christ and serve Him on this earth, Satan immediately, subtly, deftly engaged us in battle.

But there is this, victory in the name of Jesus! 2nd Corinthians reminds us, "For the weapons of our warfare are not carnal, but mighty through God, to the pulling down of strongholds." Paul and I agree: like the walls of Jericho, these strongholds of sin and Satan cannot and will not stand against the authority you can possess in Jesus Christ.

Steven Curtis
Lead Pastor/Living Faith Church - Fayetteville, Arkansas

An Endorsement from Bruce A. Jenkins

Dear Brother Paul,
I have finally found the time to read your book. The ministry of setting the captive free never seems to let up. We are having people coming from all points of the globe and especially from all over the United States. I am sorry it's taken me so long to get back to you, but, as I said. I've finally read your book. You have done an exceptional job on it. It is well thought out, and you have laid an interesting groundwork. I didn't realize what a varied and challenging life you have led. God has certainly led you to where you are now. I trust your publishing plans will soon be completed and carried out. I'm sure many people will want a copy in their arsenal on spiritual warfare. Keep in the front of the battle, my brother, the end is in sight, and the rewards for battles well fought are forthcoming.

Love in Christ, Bruce A. Jenkins

A Commendation from Best-Selling Author, Don Dickerman

This book details one man's journey in a quest for freedom from health issues and demonic oppression. Paul's determination and relentless pursuit of freedom thru Christ Jesus is encouragement for all believers."

Don Dickerman, Charisma House Author

Dedication:

≋

I dedicate this book to the Lord Jesus Christ, of Nazareth – my saving friend.

My Thanks:

≋

To those who helped me in my struggles, often giving unselfishly. As well as to those who had to put up with that previously crazy person, me.

Acknowledgment:

≋

My particular thanks to Pastor Melvin Johnson, Bro Mel. He worked with me throughout my "time of troubles," trying to deliver, heal and counsel, often-times while undergoing his trials and struggles. Those struggles are "somewhat" illustrated in this book, just in the interest of accuracy, not criticism, nothing more. I seriously doubt that Bro Mel had encountered anyone else as intensely persecuted as I was, at that time. The troubles that we were to experience as individuals while working together to defeat the demons and while working out our individual sanctifications. Sometimes involved rubbing each other smoother in that process, and this is awkward. Those times could best be viewed through the prism of demonic oppression and persecution that all in today's present-day church endure, abuse that's recognized or not, abuse that's dealt with or not! Should you in the reading of this book, decide that you need the help of the body of Christ to reveal just what is what, and help you to fuller freedom in Christ. Consider a trip to Fort Collins, Colorado, to sit before Bro Mel and submit to deliverance with a real expectation, receiving biblically sound and practical help.

Please Note:

≈≈≈

In writing this book, I've refrained from using many biblical proofs, scriptural quotations' and listings. As the books I mention and recommend in the End Notes, do that far better than me. I've done my best to keep the storyline as straight and accurate as I can. This book isn't the whole of my tale. Which in itself would have been too much, this is the meat of it, it's my story in its essentials.

As for the story itself, I didn't want to write it! One day I felt impressed to write a book about these struggles and wasn't happy about that. Then, later during prayer, I remembered a time long ago, when the Holy Spirit met and helped me with a different writing project. One from when I served with Mercy Ships on the M/V Anastasis. Back then, I used to write procurement letters and all through the whole letter writing process, I would sense the presence and recognize the help of the Holy Spirit.

While still struggling with writing this book for God. I prayed: Lord; I'll happily write this book, if, when in the writing of it. "That help of the Holy Spirit led writing-style," worked for me once again. A few weeks later, that calling was confirmed, and I went right to work. And all the while as I was typing away, the Holy Spirit would evoke memories (one's I'd suppressed) directly to the front of my mind and I typed them in. Consequently, this book is not always sequential. It mostly consists of memories, comments and reflections, my "learned lessons" from deep in the trenches of spiritual warfare.

Scriptural quotations are from the Holman HSCB
Digital Text Edition - Online Bible

On Avoiding Confusion:

≈≈≈

The storyline will be justified, indented and mostly continuous and duplicates the style of writing which you'll read in the Introduction.

My reflections and comments, will be indented and italicized and often within the storyline and in a block of text. The comments may not be chronological.

- The stronger demonic activities, those sequences, will be bulleted like the bullet to the upper left and in this size font and justified.

Commanding the spirits, will be in Bold.

Each chapter will be followed by a ***"Looking back, an Overview"*** and ***"Thoughts to take Away"*** sections. These are meant to help explain, explore and refine this book. They are intended to aid the reader in remaining in the overall flow of the story, and offer insights and comments that otherwise might be missed or just not written into the storyline itself.

Table of Contents:

Introduction. ix – xii

Book One – My autobiography, the story of my salvation and reformation, it's my redemption story. A story centered on walking in Christian missions with Mercy Ships and returning to the workforce, then - **All Hell Broke Loose!**

Book Two – My sanctification experience, the story of the all-out attacking's by the Satanic Kingdom, done in an attempt to enslave or destroy me. It's a description, an illustration and reporting on the full on spiritual warfare I endured. The sudden-onset schizophrenia, the deceptions and the story of the contest, illuminating and explaining the tools I used to obtain a final and comprehensive victory.

Book-One

A SPIRITUAL WARFARE ENSEMBLE:

Chapters 1 – 7

≈≈

Concerning this Autobiography, it's a salvation, reformation, and redemption experience. A story centered on serving in Christian missions with Mercy Ships, then returning to the workforce and subsequent events. Please see the website below for a more complete, and current understanding of this exemplary maritime ministry.

http://www.mercyships.org/

≈≈

A Strong Suggestion, if you're a "just give me the meat" style reader, or dislike detailed writing, please feel free to skip to Book Two, but you'll miss this first book's value. If nothing else, read the "Over-Views" at the chapters end. This first book contains episodes from my life experiences and illustratons of my time with Mercy Ships. The accomplishments I made there, and how the enemy was working all-the-while and unrealized, well in the background, that's its purpose.

≈≈

Overall, many others made many contributions to this tale, sometimes positively, sometimes quite the opposite; such is life. But all these "contributions" taken together, helped bring me to a lifetime crisis situation, and that is Book Two. Contributions aside, the errors and omissions are mine alone take it or leave it, it's still true and it is my story.

– Introduction –

Good day, my name is Paul Moehring; I'm 68, bald and just a mite potbellied on a thin frame. There's nothing much to see here. The fashion conscious folks routinely ignore me, and that's fine by me. Levi's jeans and direct from the dryer short sleeved shirts are my favored style. What's setting me apart from the crowd isn't the season's fashions nor the lack of them, and it's not terribly noticeable either. It's not on the outside but deep within – it's I'm a survivor; I'm still here! My Pastor once said, "Paul, of all the people I've known who've experienced the troubles you have. You're the only one who's not dead or disabled;" I just keep chugging along. When I consider that I honestly can't complain. But, - altogether, I'm a pretty happy camper. It's not that I've accomplished a lot, not as the world see's things; it's more a matter of perspective. I'm quite content now, more trusting in God and sense a deep inner peace. And what I've accomplished in life matters a lot, especially to me! I've spent years as a volunteer in emerging nations working with surgeons and medical staff, helping people without options.

I've built a mobile "lower limb" prosthetics lab in a shipping container, the first of its kind. I've helped modernize a businesses' IT structures. Some others might say, "What a complete flop! Look at him now; he's flat broke," so what? In some places, people know and appreciate me and my efforts, and in some other spots, well, not so much. These other folks, they'll need to read this to understand the severity of the headwinds I've faced, headwinds I've been buffeted by all my days. Concerning these headwinds, I know many people suffer similar things, but unfortunately. They bashfully decline help while ignoring their symptoms, failing to deal with the demonic powers opposing them! Maybe the problem lies within the church itself, where the promises of the Lord Jesus Christ are carefully and wonderfully presented. Most often without vital biblical warnings, and overlooking valid reasons why today's parishioners need heed those warnings! Have you noticed that the parables of Jesus, were frequently addressed directly to the Apostles and Disciples.

Introduction

Those parables, they surely must apply to us? Let's use for an example: the story of the virgins who were unprepared for the bridegroom's nighttime arrival, and had no oil for their lamps. Without oil, without light, they couldn't participate in the wedding feast and were cast out. Not because they were bad girls or grievous sinners, but solely, because they were unprepared. How about the parable of the wicked servant who buried the talent he'd been entrusted with, and who was afraid of failing his master. I think he made his mistake because he didn't know his master! He foolishly hid from his responsibilities out of fear, and subsequently, failed. He forfeited his chance to enter into the joy of His master and was cast out! And what about sanctification? Huh, what's that you say, sanctification? Sanctification, principally, is the purposed rejection of evil and the pursuit of the Godly. Maybe, we Christian folk we're just too busy with everyday life. Perhaps, the demons are just too subtle? What I am praying for in the writing of this book, is this. That you'll read this and see it as a guide, of sorts, an illustrated path you can identify with and follow up on. Resulting in the power and prosecution of true God, the Holy Spirit, coming against our spiritual enemies. So please use this book as an aid in your personal sanctification, in purging and growing in spiritual freedom from demons and sin. Even more importantly, I want to give all the glory to the Lord for this! For it was only by His marvelous self-sacrifice at Golgotha, from which, I obtained the power and the ability to overcome all my "personal demons," and the enemy didn't like that! Not at all; yes, thank you Lord!

Over the years I've found it odd that many obituaries are penned, discussing the merits of notable people after they've left this life in defeat. This loss is recognized as the departed person's failure to overcome their "personal-demons." Sadly, the unsaved have such a poor chance; victory is highly unlikely for them. Demons are real, and unsaved people, those without the indwelling of the Holy Spirit have no authority to oppose them! Devils and demons, they're not just a literary expression, and I don't know how to say this often enough, they're quite real! Deliverance from those demons and healing from their "demonic oppression" is available today to the Body of Christ. But, regrettably, many of us ignore our need for deliverance; despite evidence of unidentified influences in our lives, influences from spiritual forces that are foreign to us and definitely not of the Holy Spirit. Even long term Christians are at times left baffled, asking questions of themselves. Like, why couldn't I come up with a thoughtful response, back there? Or, where did that strange, accusing thought come from? That sort of rubbish. Well, read on, and you'll soon see what's likely to be happening. But don't worry, I couldn't see it coming either, not until I was under horrific demonic attack for years; three miserable years. I didn't have the information I needed back then, the information that's here! But, I was exceedingly fortunate in having some of God's Spirit-led knowledgeable people helping me: Thanks, Lord.

In the area of deliverance, Jesus said, "He came to set the captives free." He wasn't speaking of those in the local lockup but to all of us born under the reign of Lucifer in this fallen world. Jesus blazed a true path out from under the satanic, and He overpowered the demonic with his personal authority, which he now delegates to us! Jesus came to destroy the works of the devil, and He accomplished that. Utterly, completely, at the precise moment he stepped out of the grave. He destroyed the death dealing power which Lucifer had held over our heads. In the "Pastor Jenkins's Deliverance Script" (Set at Liberty) you'll find later in this book, I present a deliverance method which is not a cure all. But is a well-organized and thorough effort at a complete demonic deliverance, one which can be used by a deliverer or in self-deliverance with sound effect. Initially, you may come close to your full freedom; you may even achieve that! If not, then use this script again, starting with a fresh symptom sheet and continue on. Work with the text until the person's complete freedom is obtained, as I did for myself. It's all - very - individual! When it's done well, it's just as the Holy Spirit directs and provides for. Again, it's not a panacea. But it's the single most powerful thing I've found. As Christians, we have the Holy Spirit indwelling us, and all that Jesus accomplished in His earthly ministry working for us. That is, when we use His spiritual authority with understanding, belief, and consistency. When we fully utilize and apply these biblical truths, then, we reach our greatest authority. I'm thinking; this may be what Jesus meant. "When He said that we would go on to do greater things than He (John 14 – 12.)."

Introduction

As any spirit filled Christian can act with the authority of the Lord Jesus Christ in deliverance ministry. But all that ability is useless, entirely useless and futile, unless it's used. You have to recognize the need for using that power. Firstly using it to your own benefit. Then onto others, to fully understand this struggle for the mind and soul. It took most of my life for the circumstances and need to fall into place for this battle to commence. It had to have been the Lord's timing, His patiently waiting, aiding, directing and preparing me for this fight. It certainly wasn't my choice, and I didn't know it was coming. Back then years ago when the battle commenced, I wouldn't have found the guidance existing in this book, not yet it hadn't been penned yet. Nevertheless, this information would have helped a lot it would have been great! As it was, I was nearly blindsided, but, I endured and won full freedom; not everyone does! So please, let me guide you through my struggles, and God willing you too will learn to step out in authority, in biblical truth.

Thank you Lord Jesus Christ, that I'm alive and in good enough health to make this small contribution to your Kingdom. And am, (as far as I can realistically tell,) remarkably, entirely, demon free. Thank you that I'm working right where you want me to be, doing what you want me doing. Thanks, Lord, really. As without you, I'd be condemned and in a mental institution or under a bridge somewhere. Bless you Lord, with all my soul and all that is within me.
Amen.

End of Introduction

Chapter-One

- It's about the Iniquities -

I was born and raised in Brooklyn, New York, moving with the folks to Woodhaven Queens. At that time my older brother Walter was one of those street people you see batting at the air and mumbling to themselves. Except that Walter lived at home, that is when he wasn't institutionalized. You see I come from a demonized family. They never know this fact, and I didn't either not until much later. A little more background: I've got a mix of German and Danish blood in me. The German side wants to build the very finest, longest lasting, strongest inner tubes. But my Danish side, that side, just wants to go floating down the river in one. So I tend to go after things head down and nose to the grindstone. Then the Danish side kicks in and it's time to relax and celebrate my successes. A friend once described me as a plodder, and that's a handy way to be wired. I come from a family of plodders: fully on, or entirely relaxed, and not much in-between.

And now that I'm old, the high energy part is past me, but the concentration and willingness to engage in projects and challenging work largely remains. As I write this, I just turned sixty eight and still don't know where the time has gone. Just the other day I was twenty-five, and one of the most radical hard core bikers and law breakers around. But now, today, I'm a veteran of numerous heart attacks and some mild cancer activity. And lately I just hurt some, and my hands are starting to shake some. Years ago on a walk in Fort Collins, Colorado. I got to chat with a passing runner and he said something always hurts. I feel the pain without the bother of running! I love the Lord and work hard at trying to know and understand Him, and the things the Bible says not to neglect; I fear God. I dig deep in my mind and heart searching for explanations for the recent rocky places in my life. Also I've come to truly despise evil, and the whole satanic kingdom of Lucifer with its myriads of minions. I want to kick the slats out of it. It's a good thing there's that "Danish" side in me, or, most likely.

A Spiritual Warfare Ensemble

I'd be a real pain in the neck in my heartfelt opposition to our demonic adversaries. You see I've seen the effects of being born into this fallen world and know how merciless, cruel and powerful demonic activities and life's knocks can be. I want to expose that so hateful diabolical part. And should I do a decent job. Then maybe my learned lessons and earlier life's goofed up episodes might have some lasting value, and I find that thought very compelling. And after thinking back over my lifetime and its various events, I've decided to write this book starting from my teenage years onward.

It's been a bit of a mystery to me on how to communicate what I've been given. What I've endured, and what I've gained from all this, and the addressing of that begins here.

≈≈≈

I left home shortly after my High School Graduation in 1963, joining the US Navy. It wasn't much of an escape but it was an escape nonetheless, and that was the whole point. I just wanted to get out of there! During my teenage years my brother Walter was reluctantly, painfully, becoming clinically insane. It was about then that he endured the first of his psychiatric commitments. My folks were nominal Christians, and there wasn't much in the way of deliverance available way back then. Even if they had known to look for this manner of healing. All they undertook in desperately trying to help were those days' "standard psychological treatments," which were debilitating and unhelpful. Treatments consisting of electric shock therapy and psychotropic drugs. Walter faced these things bravely and well, sometimes even asking for further treatment, but it did him no good, none at all. Meanwhile in the US Navy, I served aboard an old Landing Ship Tank from WWII, an LST. One of those vessels you see in the D-Day footage - troops coming down the bow-ramps and jeeps and tanks coming out of the splayed open bow-doors. Most often, we were going up and down the muddy rivers of Vietnam, working with the 9th Marines Expeditionary Force. Even at that young age I was a screw-up. It seemed like I always managed to pick the wrong thing to do, I had no discipline then; because I wasn't raised with any. That's just how it was; I was cannon fodder for demons from a demonized family.

2

But really, almost all our families have their spiritual liabilities, and particularly their iniquities in operation. To help illustrate how this works. I remember one sunny day when our LST-854, the Kemper County was sailing up the Saigon River. An ugly brown river that snakes and undulates its way through thick and thicker mangrove swamps. We rounded one bend and happened on a small harbor class oil tanker, sprouting flame and taking Vietcong fire. I was on deck supporting the firefighters sent onboard, struggling and working to douse the fires and prepare it for towing. As the scene unfolded, I was sheltering under the starboard bridge wing aft on the main deck, and from there I began evaluating the Vietcong's incoming fire. My first thought was, "they sure were lousy shots." So, I decided all I had to do was avoid standing next to whatever they were shooting at, and I'd be OK. Well, maybe that wasn't such a smart idea, but the idea fit comfortably. So I did whatever I needed to with little regard for the enemy firing away. Hmm, I wonder where those thoughts came from, and why they fit so well and so subtly, powerfully compelling me. Some years later, I saw a TV show on people's reactions to danger. One example they showed was a British soldier, unconcernedly strolling along the beach during the English Army's June 1940 Dunkirk evacuation. While the beach was ferociously dive-bombed! You could hardly see the water for the bobbing dead men. Corpses all over the place and other troopers furiously digging foxholes. I wasn't alone in simply ignoring death and injury's distinct possibility; there were others foolishly convinced of their invulnerability, a fantasy, sure we all know that, but what was staging this?

There was something going on here, something that I was not to learn of until much later in life. One minute more please, let me work on this just a bit more.

There are three kinds of sin most commonly committed. Firstly is the sin of "trespass," where you knowingly do something wrong. Next, the sin of "omission," where you didn't do what you knew you should have. The third sin seldom gets an explanation and is immensely powerful, "iniquity."

Iniquity is the sin of the unbeliever, it's the often secret unforgiven sins of the fathers, passed on to the third and fourth generation of those that hate God. The consequences of this sin are passed on into the family's bloodline. Sometimes by an altered DNA as science observes and if you wish. Or, almost always by demons! Iniquities are the original and deepest roots of one's "demonic oppression." To explain further, I once saw a show on PBS about the household of the sixth US president, John Quincy Adams. The story was about his family history, in comparison to the clan across the tracks. The Adams family was Christian, socially responsible and spiritually alive. The other family was spiritually defunct, lacking, longing and socially disastrous. The Adams family produced several US presidents, state senators, college deans, doctors etc. and grew with each new generation. The other family produced several horse thieves and some failed businesses; usually living unremarkable lives. Then came lawsuits, some bankruptcies, and they were scarcely getting by, they barely managed to remain a family. That show was supposed to have demonstrated the healthy influence of Christianity on families. But, what they actually illustrated were iniquities at work. In the Christian family, as the family members followed the Lord and did right in God's sight iniquities were dealt with. That's part of the protection afforded children born into Godly families. Across the road, nada. It was an example of full on consequences in action. My family was more like the family across the tracks. So when my brother and I were born, iniquities applied, and immediately, right at conception!

These generational encumbrances are applicable to any- body's child, excepting those children born with a great & good fortune of being heir to successful families. Families that had followed the Lord, like father like son.

Since I've learned about iniquities I've changed. I've lost my old options and cannot reject anyone anymore. Sometimes, people don't stand much of a chance Christian or not. Our world is a broken and seriously damaged world, and its diverse peoples too often live under the prince of this world. So having lived long enough to gain a bit of understanding of how life in this fallen world often functions.

It's about the Iniquities

It seems to me that only Jesus has the right to judge. Only He can see the actual condition of one's heart and understand all the bits and pieces to a life. The greatest part of this is, in Exodus 20: 5-6, in one translation it says, "But showing love to a thousand generations of those who love me and keep my commandments."

"Looking back, an Overview"

~~~

Today, being wonderfully free and looking back. I can see that, yes, I am entirely responsible for how I've lived, every little bit of it. Even now, after experiencing lots of demonic hurdles, there's still no excuse for immorality or irresponsibility. We'll all live or die daily by our thoughts - our decisions behind our deeds. We must give an account for it all; one day, soon enough. Even so, with all the varied worldly influences, the traps, and the subtle compulsions laid on us by our spiritual enemies, the demons. Surely these things must play a role in our choices. But - how strong a role?

That depends on our resistance or acquiesce to them and our awareness of their tricks. It's a wonderful thing that we serve a just God. Sorting all that out is far beyond me!

"Thoughts to take Away"

~~~

Young parents, please pay attention. So your children don't have to go through all I did! Even though, we're now aware of these inherited iniquities, a legacy you certainly didn't wish for. But one which, exposes the roots of many daily struggles. You're still entirely responsible for your thoughts, your deeds, or the lack of them.

So please be aware of the distinct possibility of your harboring inherited iniquities in your bloodline. Then know that you and the Lord working together can destroy them all, freeing you and generations to come from their injurious effects.

Chapter-Two

- Old life, new Life -

On returning to the US from Vietnam, with my mind filled full with left over military nonsense, distilled from the crass naval culture. Along with some disturbing and fresh memories. There was then, a bit of confusion working away. You see the war in Vietnam wasn't on the national radar when I enlisted, I hadn't even heard of South Vietnam, back when - who had? So serving there came as a rather unpleasant surprise to me. Consequently as I reflected on my recent experience's I came to a quite particular conclusion: and this was. That if my government could send me wholly unprepared to dangerous places, and more importantly. Send me there for someone else's civil war? Screw them all. I was going to do whatever I felt like, let them try and catch me. Yup, full on rebellion was in operation then, it just came naturally bubbling up to the surface. There were many reasons I had disliked the Naval Service, including the fact that I didn't need it. I made my own living (one I enormously enjoyed) in the civilian sector. I was working part time at every chance I could get, for a bike shop in downtown San Diego, California. That interest shifted to full time employment at my enlistment's end.

My interest in fast motorcycles and fast women was rather intense, and I wound up a few years later as an officer in the Outlaw's M/C, Motorcycle Club that is. Outlaw bikers are an intriguing group although a tad-bit self destructive. The drugs, excessive law breaking lifestyle, the occasional violence and somewhat slippery tires of the day, were a pretty incendiary stew. A woman who had been praying for me once remarked, "Angels must have had a hard time keeping you alive." And that was probably true, it was fun though. Principally, my joining the motorcycle club was an example of the snap decisions I made and stiff consequences I had to pay, penalties that were to last for decades. Behavior whose root causes I had no clue of or desire or the means to investigate in those days. The result of this "outlaw biker guy" nonsense, was a long string of arrests and occasional trials, and no, they never caught me in a felony.

A Spiritual Warfare Ensemble

I had many off color and drug induced adventures, many of which would eventually be pretty funny stories. But I was wasting my life and all my potential.

Time for a story, there were two Outlaw chapters; mine in San Diego, CA. and the other in Los Angeles. After a few days of carousing in LA.with brother Outlaws and the Barons a motorcycle social club. Whose clubhouse was Rudolph Valentino's old mansion; a huge half block sized multistoried and domed psychedelic party house in LA Central. We decided to organize a run to New York City, hoping to see the "Tall Ships" coming into port for the Nation's 200th Anniversary. A week later, a half dozen of us were on the way to Phoenix Arizona, to recruit a friend for the ride named Doc. At the time my club name was Moe, and I was riding a highly modified and quite fast 750 cc Norton Scrambler motorcycle, I like sweet running machines. After a three hundred mile charge across the desert we arrived at Doc's house. And kicked back to start partying with pot and whatever drugs were handy or stashed on the bikes. Later on, we all got the munchies. At the time, we were running scams to keep money coming in, and I happened to be the only one with any cash that day, so off Doc and I went off to the supermarket. One of the guys on the ride was named Aig, pronounced, "Egg." Aig was stocky, completely bald in his early forties, and sported a Fu Manchu mustache and goatee. Aig smoked more pot in a day than anyone else I knew did in a week. Aig was an exceptionally talented dope dealer and conman, a great guy, and a lot of fun. With Aig in mind at the market, I filled a large bag with goodies. Then, I had a thought. I went back and started another bag. This one had a gallon of apple juice, a box of matzos and a couple packs of butter. Returning to the house, I left the big bag in the car and proudly placed the little one on the floor by Aig, and then broke out all my goodies. Aig was perplexed and mystified. Then, as he tried the matzos with a smearing of butter and a tall glass of apple juice, flat out enraged. Moe, this is awful, you no good rotten and other various cussing's and mutterings, and so on, as I let him stew for a while. Then I got the large bag from the car, and Aig just huffed and complained to himself. It was good fun. This type of thing was nearly constant in the club. We were always playing pranks, some innocent like my groceries, and some were purely hazardous. The run continued, with the pack in different stages various levels of intoxication. We rarely rode more

than three hundred miles a day, before we set up camp and par-
tied. Eventually, we made our way to Pittsburgh Pennsylvania,
with delays to party with other bikers, run a quick scam, spend
a few days in jail and work some odd jobs, etc. One evening, I
was partying with some guys in the back of a Van. There were
good sized bowls of hashish making their rounds, but I was
bored with getting stoned. I jabbed the guy on my right, asking if
he wanted to see Aig go berserk. He thought for a moment and
said, "Sure, why not?" I leaned forward, caught Aig's eye and
said, "hey Aig; Matzos!" Aig went nuts, arms flailing in the air,
feet bouncing off the floor. Aig lamented; I hate matzo's, nasty,
butter slimy, crumbling nothing tasting, Moe you rotten, misera-
ble, and on and on. Aig's blistering, anti-matzo tirade, ran every-
one out of the Van except for me and this guy on my right. We
were laughing so hard I thought I might crack a rib. Aig was a
great guy.

Outlaw bikers rarely stay active in a club more than seven or
eight years, and I sensed my time as an Outlaw was drawing to a close.
Things were just not right within the club. There were too many difficulties between the club's brothers and the Outlaws had buried several
members who were close friends of mine. And I was wondering if this
Outlaw lifestyle could possibly be worth it. The last straw came as I
was doing a brief stint in the San Diego City Jail. There was a friendly
cop there that I knew, and he warned me that they (the San Diego PD)
had tired of my act and were looking to set me up. Adding it all up, I
decided to take a hard look at myself and check to see what prospects
I might have. I soon realized that I had few indeed and decided to
make changes. I knew I needed to get back to school and get a fresh
start.

Circumstances piled up, and I saw an opportunity to hon-
orably withdraw from the Outlaws and did so. But the best and
only valuable thing coming from my life as a biker occurred some
decades later, and it came from my salvation. After I had my in-
itial salvation experience and as I began to grow as a Christian
on looking back over my life until then. I wanted to be sure my
old friends didn't miss out on the same opportunity that I had
embraced, that of asking for Jesus's forgiveness. And prayed
fervently, and often for my old biker buddies, some of whom were
genuinely close friends.

"Looking back, an Overview"

≈≈≈

Some decades later, Brian Melvin, a compelling biblical exposi-
tor and a fellow parishioner at All Nations Church in Fort Col-
lins, Colorado, would occasionally speak at our church. Brian
had authored a book about trials he'd experienced in his life en-
titled, "A Land Unknown: Hell's Dominion." It goes like this,
some years ago; he was revived from an "after death" experi-
ence. He'd died of Cholera and was dead for about four hours,
during that time he went straight to Hell. While there, Brian
was rescued by the Lord Jesus Christ and received a guided
tour of the place. He then woke up in an ICU, incredibly terri-
fied. He wrote a book about his experiences nearly thirty years
ago, and his book was just recently published. It took him that
long to get his mind around it, and on occasion, he'd tell us ta-
les of his after death experiences. At a Wednesday night bible
study. I was relating an opinion about how demons can inter-
ject their thoughts into your mind. When Brian spoke up making
an insightful comment. He told us that while he was in Hell
He'd seen demons sitting on poles, singing songs of self de-
struction, assaulting people's thoughts, hammering them with
music based on self destructive themes. That harmonized with
my explanation on how demons can inject a thought into your
mind, unnoticed, by starting with a question and answering it
themselves. You'd think the entire thought string was your own,
spoken by your own internal voice, when no part of it was from
you at all! I'd occasion to wonder what part the demonic may
have played in my thinking processes. I'd wondered about that
for a long time, what could be going on I'd wondered? Long be-
fore I became a Christian at age thirty-nine. Why had I made
such poor choices? Why had I become a biker, way back when?
It was an experience I barely survived. Could Brian's revela-
tions and mine now, help to explain it?

"Thoughts to take Away"

≈≈≈

Blaming demons for everything wrong in your life, that's just not realistic. What's partly to blame is our flesh (what the Jews in Jesus's day, called the "evil inclination.") Then this fallen world we live in, and evil supernaturalism all combined! These enemies plot and probe, it's their very nature. Demonically organized to subtly, powerfully, affect our everyday life long experiences. They're working to keep the unsaved out of the Kingdom, and to shipwreck those within.

The demons are just one facet of the problem of living Godly lives in a fallen world. The trick lies in learning to recognize when something in your head or heart needs to be investigated. You'll need to identify its source, and then, decide if you must deal with it. And from there it's all about – just how to do that! – It's called the process of Sanctification.

Chapter-Three

- Salvation and Onward -

Leaving the Outlaws behind, I initiated my own "fresh start-self rescue program." And that brought me to Los Angeles California, for a two year dental laboratory course at a college there. I reasoned that I could learn that business and open a lab on a shoestring, all by utilizing "on the job training," I'd make my own apprenticeship. That was my focus for the next decade. I moved to different states, to more eastern cities, one's where I had no local arrest records, and worked at the labs I found there. As I became quite skilled in one area of the trade I would change jobs. At the new lab, I'd work in a skill area that was new to me claiming to be a little rusty. And I'd work like a beaver learning that new skill and only staying until I'd learned it thoroughly. I was continuously working to develop my skill set. I persisted until I learned the craft well enough to open my very own Crown and Bridge Dental Lab in San Antonio, Texas. Overall, I had worked in a half dozen or so places, in Texas, Colorado Springs, Colorado, and in New York City.

Without owning a crown and bridge lab, I wasn't going to learn the management side. So, I went and did it, I opened my very own! But then something else occurred, something truly extraordinary!

Before starting my lab, I'd made a friend named Neil at my last job, and he was a Christian. Neil encouraged me to check out his church, Christ Redeemer Church and see what I thought. He said there were some cute nurses there. So off to church Neil and I went. The church was in a shared building then, leased from the city in a public park. It was a very pleasant setting. I thought worship there was quite strange; I saw people talking in tongues, babbling and talking nonsense like crazy people. The songs were new to me and kind of different but energizing. And the hand clapping's and such behavior was all very new and strange to me. I wasn't at all sure of what to think about all of that, but then, there was this kind of light there.

This light wasn't incandescent or fluorescent; it was everywhere and nowhere, subtly encompassing. I've always enjoyed architecture so I went hunting for the light source but couldn't find it, not even close. The following week I returned to Christ Redeemer Church, determined to find that light. Where was it coming from? By the third Sunday I had decided it just didn't matter, and I wasn't going back. It was still curious though. While thinking about this church and my going there. I realized that had I continued on I'd have been obliged to abandon my vices and old biker style thinking. And to retire my old attitudes and look for something else something new, and I'd wondered about that. A few days later, Neil, gave me a package while at work in a plain brown wrapping. I took the curious bundle home to discover a Bible inside. Huh? Quite intrigued, I started reading, searching for something the pastor had said, "Something about Jesus being our champion." I instinctively knew I needed a champion. I read the entire book of Romans, then Ephesians, then John, but still couldn't find that phrase. Even so, while engaged in reading that Bible I realized that sins, serious ones, one's that would keep me from entering heaven would be forgiven, if I just asked.

Later that night in bed reading the Bible on my chest, I remember quietly asking the Lord Jesus to please forgive me, and fell fast asleep. On the following day, I awoke from the most restful sleep I'd ever known. I walked towards the bathroom, glanced in the mirror, and did a double take. I saw myself strikingly aglow and a-washed with light clean from the inside out. I remember thinking, "it's a good thing I've been around the block once or twice or I wouldn't believe this!" This was amazing. And my emotions, boy, they were hugely affected and incredibly noticeable. I completely understood what peace, joy, contentment, and acceptance meant. My definitions for those words had been radically changed, and I had a new outlook on life. I'd never felt such pure, intense emotions before. And I wasn't to experience such feelings at that full intensity, not again that is. Not until the Lord gave me another such, wonderfully vivid - spiritual experience which I will write about later. After soaking in all this, I had to get into the days necessary things and prepared for work. When I walked into the dental lab I worked for then, everyone's mouth fell open.

And they put their heads down not saying a word. That glow, quite pronounced at first lasted for several days. I told everyone there what had happened to me, but they didn't have anything to say and looked rather puzzled. I thought it likely they'd not enjoyed a similar experience, and my experience wasn't anything they could relate to, not yet. I wore out that presentation Bible over the next few weeks hunting for answers to questions like: "just who is this Jesus guy?" And "if He's God like I'd heard, then who is He praying to?" which is still, a pretty fair question, I think. The next year or so was a time of intense exploration for me. I was working to find out what was what. The Bible was my constant companion; I'd settle in to read it and the Holy Spirit would just light up the words as I read it. I had a friend in the past who'd become a Jehovah's Witness and used to come by and leave me things to read. But at no time was there any revelations like this. Their stuff was dry as a bone it was empty. But when I read my bible, scripture after scripture would light up for me, it was like the very words on the page would glow. They were that alive to me, and I understood those words at a deep, gut level.

Often, during that time, I would find myself torn up with regret when I remembered my past sins. I used to wonder how I could be of any use to God. This God who had saved me, especially after all my rebellious episodes, a life that was still such a mess. It was a shame then, but I couldn't appreciate all of my blessings. I walked quite closely with the Holy Spirit, and when I prayed, it was as if I could get out of the way and the Holy Spirit used my mouth for His speech. His words would pour through me, and people would look at each other. Or shake their heads and say something like, "now that's the way to pray!" As for me, I didn't know what was happening. Christianity was a brand new exciting experience, and there weren't any classes I knew of, one's that would introduce me to the ways of God. When I tried to talk with long time Christians about my experiences, some would say "leave those things to the mystics," whatever that meant. Sometimes and often at unexpected moments, I'd be praying, and it was like there was a swirling gray, blue, and red streaked cloud, slowly revolving and forming over my head. I could see it in my mind's eye, and the Holy Spirit would so softly thrust me into a fetal position.

And I would find myself trying to throw up what I pictured as a nasty black ball, which was stuck somewhere deep, deep inside the bowels of my heart. Unfortunately, I didn't succeed in getting that thing out. I believe those experiences were some direct demonic deliverance from the Holy Spirit. It was deliverance that I would experience at various times over the next few years.

Before my salvation, I would often sit on the porch, considering the worsening world situation, and I became increasingly concerned about my spiritual condition. I reasoned that I was sure to go to Hell and well deserved it. But that thought deeply troubled me. One day, when I was thinking about these things I suddenly got a thought. "That I ought to kill myself and get it over with." That thought seriously alarmed me as it didn't feel right, like it wasn't my own. I'm not a coward in very many things. So, where did the idea of suicide come from? It so shocked me that I think that this incident played a persuasive role in my checking out Neil's Church. I believe this proves the popular saying, "that what the devil meant for evil, the Lord used for my good" is a good and valid one.

About seven or eight months after my salvation, I was in my lab working when a magazine showed up in the mail. I hadn't ordered it; I didn't send for it, I didn't recognize it. But I was quite intrigued and excited while thumbing through this magazine, and also, (this was extremely curious to me) I wondered why I was so intrigued and excited about it? This was quite peculiar. It was a Christian Missions Catalog an odd thing to have just shown up. I started reading through it in detail, instead of just skimming and thought it quite unlikely that it would have anything for me. I was a dental lab guy. Where would a dental lab in San Antonio, Texas, fit in Christian Missions? At the very back of the magazine, I noticed a small advertisement for Mercy Ships. Would a ship, especially a larger ship, be one of the few places in missions where a dental lab could be operated? At times, I still wondered how the Lord could use a guy like me. Now, here was this mission's magazine. What was going on? I felt I'd better call the number, and so I did reaching Mercy Ships Headquarters. I was told to call the ship; it was in Canada at the shipyards undergoing modifications and upgrades. I called the number in Canada.

16

A man came on the line and introduced himself as Dr. Richard Ruhe, and asked how he could help me? I asked him, had they any need for dental lab services? There was a moment's hesitation, and he replied "We just got through praying about that." Oh-boy! I was to learn later that the department had been energetically praying and petitioning the Lord for more staff. It seems God does work in mysterious ways! And so, I was off to speak with my pastor, leader of the church of the subtle and intriguing light, mentioned earlier. We discussed this, and I told him I'd already booked a flight to Canada to see what might be in store for me. I thought that if this was genuine and of the Lord then maybe there was an opportunity here. Perhaps it was a chance for me to be of some service in the Lord's kingdom. Something just for me, a rather gnarly ex-biker and former ne'er-do-well to do in response to my saving God. But my pastor got a bit aggravated and declared. "You've been a church member for a short time, and there was no way the church was going to support you for the rest of your life." The whole thing sounded a bit off to him and he said, "You might have it all wrong and fail."

My thought was, if I failed to exert myself in trying to follow the Lord then I would have failed right from the outset! I told him that he might be right. But I'd already booked the flight and had barely enough funds for the trip, (dental labs billed monthly, and it was late in the month). And so I said that, "I honestly thought this could be of God, and I needed to pay attention." I heard later that he changed his mind deciding that I had the right attitude after all. A friend told me this conversation became the basis of a sermon he gave while I was in Canada; I'd guess it was after some quiet reflection. The flight was in three legs and once on the ground a crewmember with an old and struggling car, drove me and some other visitors to the Esquimalt Shipyard. Then to the berth where Mercy Ship's - (Motor Vessel) – the M/V Anastasis was tied up. The Esquimalt Shipyard is in Victoria, a beautiful city that is the provincial capital of British Columbia. I know about ships from working in shipyards and from reading and naval service. And as we pulled into the shipyard, the QE2 was berthed alongside a pier and was ablaze with light. She was a seventy thousand ton floating palace!

17

It was gorgeous, and the others got all excited, but I thought nah that couldn't be. I looked around, and further down the yard at another pier was an old and weathered looking ship with a few dim yellow lights. It was somewhat rusted but had elegant lines, lines of an older generation. Yup, that was the M/V Anastasis. Twelve thousand tons, one hundred fifty eight feet long, fifty eight feet wide, and nine decks tall. The last riveted hull, Cargo and Passenger Liner anywhere. A tough and worn survivor the last of its kind. Next day, I met Dr. Ruhe and Cynthia his Dental Assistant, and was given a tour. Some of the ship's spaces were filthy. They had just finished a massive project installing a ship wide pressurized sprinkler system. The vessel had predated the requirement for such a system but time had caught up with them, and the US Coastguard declared the system as necessary for sailing to First World ports. It had been an arduous two year's installation, done by volunteers and very little money just grit and determination. They'd succeeded admirably, and now the final cleanup was getting underway.

At the end of the tour, Richard showed me a small room at the pointy end of B-deck, one deck below the Reception Desk (on A-Deck) at the ship's entrance and forward in the bows of the ship, port (or left side.) It had been the ship's carpenter shop, and Richard humbly presented the space. Saying this was the location for a projected dental lab. When he asked what I thought. I said that it was about everything I was afraid it might be! It contained an old wooden vise, an antique that used wedges to clamp wooden objects in place. There were holes in the plastered walls, insulation showing through. The ships ribs prominently displayed through the walls, along with paint sprays and gouges typical to a work area. The room was 4 ½' wide, X - 9' long. X - 3 ½' wide, near the bow at the floor level. It looked like a carpenter's shop would. The outer wall (the hull) had a decent curve outwards in this part of the ship. So, it was about fifteen inches wider overhead, and it did have a porthole and one flat straight wall aft and a door opening onto the B-Deck passageway. Such passageways surrounded the ship's cargo holds and engineering spaces. The vessel was a bit of a rabbit warren, but all ships are. Richard asked me to pray and think about it and stay in touch.

"Looking back, an Overview"

≈≈≈

The odd part of this early history of mine, and then later, salvation. Was the amount of demonic interference and the subtlety of it all? I had no idea of the extent of the oppression I experienced; I was so accustomed to it all.

It was as though, that through my lack of discipline and the absence of clear direction. The flesh was not only in charge. But was rooted on and ably assisted by otherworldly powers. And despite all that life long and quite intense opposition, prayers prayed for me ultimately triumphed. Thank God.

"Thoughts to take Away"

≈≈≈

Over and over again I see this pattern. Instead of the sins of the past; I'm dead to such sins now. Those overt sins of commission they're rare now. Today, I find I need to stay on the lookout for those sins of omission! That's far and away the toughest one, the subtle killer of Christian virtue. I must walk with the Lord with no deviations allowed. The consequences of not doing so are just too tough.

Chapter-Four

- The M/V Anastasis -

Having seen the Anastasis and finding out that it was about what I expected and was a bit leery of. I figured that if I were smart, I shouldn't be the only one making a decision about this missionary lab opportunity. I reasoned I needed to hear strongly, and directly from the Lord Himself. So, it was back to basics in San Antonio, and I prayed, fasted, and then prayed some more, then a bit more. About six weeks later, while reading the Bible one weekend afternoon. I heard from somewhere deep in my heart, the book, chapter, and verse of a scripture. It was what I'd been praying for, and it gave me some definite direction. I was to look to Mercy Ships for the next stage of my life. A short time later, I became convinced that I was to enroll in the Discipleship Training School, a (DTS) held aboard the M/V Anastasis. This DTS was the first step in "Youth with a Mission's" process to be in Christian missions with Mercy Ships, which was then a principal YWAM ministry. A successful completion of the DTS would help win the ministries approval for constructing a full service dental lab aboard the Anastasis.

But, there was this nagging thought, an odd check that I'd noticed, and it made me wonder. It happened on my entrance into the Anastasis. The precise moment I stepped on the ship itself it felt like some internal lights just went out. It was quite evident. Ever since I'd been saved until that very moment, I'd enjoyed a sense of profound peace and that had been disturbed. It was like I'd lost touch with a dear friend. I asked Dr. Ruhe, the dentist, about that odd feeling, and he said that some other visitors had mentioned similar experiences. He seemed confused by the whole thing. Nowadays this doesn't seem so strange to me. Let me take a moment to explain: years later, early in my process of deliverance from nonstop demonic attacks. Cindy Richards a deliverer at my church, once said that she saw a ship and spirits that came out of this vessel's holds, to attack and enter me. And this was before I'd said a word to her about Mercy Ships. These were spirits of death and madness, vicious and malign spirits.

A Spiritual Warfare Ensemble

It turned out there were many spirits that had been oppressing me from that old and much traveled ship. The M/V Anastasis had been with Mercy Ships for some years then. It had been to the South Sea Islands and South and Central America. She'd brought light, spiritual healing, and healthful Christian attitudes. Salvation's occurred, and equipment and supplies went to port cities that were otherwise strongly under the cruel control of their territorial spirits. And those spirits had fought back! What doesn't surprise me now is this, even though some individuals had recognized there was something spiritually out-of-kilter on that ship. No one undertook to clean up the mess; it was a real shame. It would have been quite difficult, but not impossible. As so often happens in this life, it's all about priorities and energy and time, and crewmembers usually spent from that day's activities.

I remember once, being awakened in the middle of the night with a vision from the Holy Spirit. A scene in full color, depicting a shaman sitting outside his hut, the fire was going it was hot and humid sweat coursed down his torso, figurines were present and incantations were at work. Energetically and enthusiastically, he cursed and cursed. That sort of thing had been at work in various places, directed at that ship and the people on it. To continue on; it took about eight months to raise funds for the shipboard Discipleship Training School. I put in lots of long hours those days, working hard to pay off debts and struggled with Infernal Revenue taxes.

Incidentally, I was still moving forward in my walk with God, I'd been reading the Word and studying books about the Word, working diligently, trying to know the Lord better. After attending a weeklong Bill Gothard Bible Conference. I remember thinking about the honesty, integrity, and truthfulness of scripture and wondered where it might apply in my life, and the Holy Spirit showed up! I saw scenes of familiar yet strange looking places. I remember having a bird's eye view of a landscape in grayscale, mostly of shadows and shapes, mountains and meadows. In appearance, it was not unlike a scene you would see at night. Say from a train while going through deep passes in the Rocky Mountains. I understood it to be a glimpse of another place, perhaps another dimension. I was given an awareness that there truly is "something more." Also, there was a sort of weight, and I felt as though I was being pressed into the mattress. Then, I began speaking in tongues. Not gibberish, but another language with context and structure, I just didn't know what the words meant. Lastly, I remember celebrating this extraordinary experience by becoming overjoyed and energized. Knowing that God was real and rewards those who diligently seek Him. That had been the theme of the conference. My relationship with the Lord Jesus had been good and was beginning to get better. I had lots of joy in the Lord and excitement about life and was looking forward to the DTS.

In case you're unfamiliar with my expressions and what is meant by them, salvation, being "saved:" most people recognize as a notable, memorable, life changing spiritual experience. It's the first day's foot in the door initial experience of Christianity, which leads towards greater faith. That faith is developed and proven over time. Conversion, often, is a secondary spiritual experience, a further filling out. In some denominations it's recognized as the Baptism of the Holy Spirit. It's when a "saved, believing" Christian has responded to the Lord and has sought out further knowledge of God's ways. The Holy Spirit responds to this with a spiritual baptizing. It's His action, not yours. It's His response to a right heart attitude. It's an additional "fleshing out," an equipping for service of a believing Christian.

I showed up for the DTS School in October 1987, at the Esquimalt shipyard, Victoria, BC. Victoria is the beautiful, historical, capital city of British Columbia. Canada's Pacific Ocean maritime province. I was to spend seven years on the M/V Anastasis starting from there. During the first year, there was completing the DTS then building the dental lab. As always there were many lessons to learn. The DTS speakers were a series of pastors and Christian workers from all over the planet. They spoke on many different subjects, centering on serving Christ and His Kingdom, powerfully teaching on who God is and how to get along with Him and honor each other. This school was an introduction to Christianity I would have loved to have undertaken earlier. Then there was evangelism, and an outreach to Mexico. First Mexico City then the port city of Lazaro Cárdenas.

This "DTS Outreach" was followed by a break back in Texas with a friend of whom I'll write about later, Rob Joy, and time to report as crew. At that point, I began the task of building the dental lab, equipping it from my stored equipment and supplies, and then operating it in various ports. That lab saw service in Mexico and the Caribbean and in West Africa, also Eastern and Western Europe, and in the Baltic Sea. Something like fifteen countries and thirty plus port cities in the years I was aboard. During outreaches, I would make artificial eyes, ears, dental appliances, and hybrid facial parts. Sometimes I got to see the surgical patients that were wearing my oral appliances, installed by the ship's maxillo-facial surgeon. Those devices held the surgical and dental restructurings in place as they healed from their surgeries. Young men with severely deformed faces were now nice looking everyday folks, instead of the local rejects. It was a gratifying result for people previously ashamed of themselves. People who'd been hiding or covering their deformities. The results I saw were terrific, really encouraging. Off outreach, I worked with the crew and the ship's dentists.

"Looking back, an Overview"

≈≈

Currently, I'm in the second season of my life where I have packed up or disposed of all my stuff to prepare to serve in missions. In both instances the struggles presented themselves and took center stage. But on this second time around, in the midst of all the chores and the work and the many trips to the dumpster, things have changed. Without the demonic oppression I can now walk away from my "difficulties," regroup with the Lord, and do what I am called to do with peace and joy.

The first time around in missions, the cost in practical terms for my service with Mercy Ships was high. However, I remain pleased with my accomplishments and am grateful for my time there, valuing the friends and memories made.

"Thoughts to take Away"

≈≈

Efforts spent in serving the Lord give us seasons of quality time with Him, extra fine time. Attaining that elusive "quality time," is not such a simple thing. But a big piece of the puzzle on how to do that is personal sanctification. We need to be engaged in the business of destroying demonic obstacles and blockages to our ties to Jesus Christ. We do this so we can walk in real peace and joy.

- The cost is insignificant, compared to the benefits.-

Chapter-Five

- My poor brother Walter -

A fter three outreaches to the Dominican Republic, the Anastasis toured in the United States. She was doing support raising and public relations and opened herself up for public tours. I took the opportunity then to visit my Dad. The M/V Anastasis was going to sail for West Africa shortly, and he was not doing so well. I visited for a while before the ship left and thought he'd be fine, but a satellite call over the Atlantic soon disproved that. I took a flight back to New York from Scotland and a leave of absence so I could tend to my father. Dad was an exceptionally good man. He was a trustworthy father and provider to my brother and me. And, I'm well assured he was a loving husband and the lifelong friend of my Mom. (After she died, he truly missed his best friend.) I tried to help him understand how to have a closer relationship with the Lord, and soon realized that in his own way he did know God, but not in the same manner as me.

A word of explanation here. It's not strange to me now, now that I understand how it worked. But, try as I might back then. It was not possible for me to ask Dad in the "classic evangelical" style of: "Hey Dad, do you want to know the Lord Jesus Christ as your savior?" The words just wouldn't form. My thoughts would take flight, and I'd soon realize a moment had passed that would have been better utilized. It was those darned demons. That's how they work; they'd block and scatter thoughts like a thumb over a garden hose's nozzle. Splitting and diverting thoughts like turning a stream of water into a spray and water splatter, they messed things up. The Holy Spirit, my strengthener and friend, assured me that my Dad was a part of the Body of Christ despite the demons. That's how He works.

During Dad's lifetime, the church he'd known had been pretty dry so he remained a nominal Christian and didn't get much involved. In discussing Jesus and the Bible with Dad, I knew the bonds were there - the ones between Christians that are a part of the body of Christ. He was a part of the body, and I am so grateful for that, it's a reassurance I treasure to this day.

Dad died on a sunny day, asking for more light as Voltaire had. He slipped into a coma, passing away while safe at home. I was proud of him as he went out with dignity and love, and I miss him to this day. In the months prior to his death, I had gotten to know him better. We'd grown close, Dad and me. My Brother's earlier trials and presence had prevented that, long before I left for the Navy. Dad was of a quiet and steady generation, not given to much emotional expression. It was funny; he and I were talking once, and he happened to mention that one of his big regrets was that he never wrote me when I was in Vietnam. I would call home from someplace now and then, but being from a demonized family I missed a lot and just didn't realize it, and never would. Not until I'd gotten free of the things. After Dad passed on I had a small funeral for him. My Brother Walter came, but he didn't understand. It was like Walter lacked any understanding of what Dad's death should mean for him. He didn't know how to take the reality of it. After the funeral services, Walter came to the house from the adult hotel where he was living and flopped on the couch. He stretched, groaned, and gave a whopping sigh of relief.

Now he could do some serious couch warming and fantasizing. (Schizophrenics often live in a fantasy world, one of intricate staged plays and self-centered heroics). And now without the old man's unwanted distracting presence. I sent him back to his hotel so I could grieve without this foolishness. He fantasized that he could now just eat, drink, and lay about indefinitely. Without realizing that his Dad (his provider and protector) was gone, and he was on his own for the very first time. Walter was a full blown schizophrenic and mildly emotionally retarded. He had some physical problems but what ruined and ruled him were demons. He was a house to scads and scads of demons; many picked up from his institutions. Over the years psychotic drugs had destroyed Walter's nerves; he couldn't even grasp things. Physically he was a wreck, mentally a mess, and was a hugely tormented individual. But, like many psychotic folks he had his fantasies and in them he was king of the world. That great guy and hero stuff, that lasted until the crash, and there was always a crash after the highs. Then, the demons would come mocking and tormenting him. It was an entirely wasted and miserable life.

My poor brother Walter

Just recently, I was watching a "Ted" show which featured a speaker at a conference for neurologists and psychologists. The speaker's schizophrenic brother had prompted her career as a neurologist and brain researcher. She grew up trying to understand her brother and his "disease." Oddly enough, she too endured a schizophrenic attack from which she eventually recovered. The experience caused her to dig deeply into researching the human brain. She described brain functioning with the left globe, the right, and its various parts. Also, she explained how thoughts are put together and managed by the brain. It was so aggravating to watch this show. Because what she was unwittingly describing was how demonic spirits could disrupt and disorganize a person's thinking, including her own! I especially remember her explaining how she woke up one morning suddenly schizophrenic, just like her brother, and she didn't even recognize it as an attack. To her it seemed as if this was something temporary, something to just be worked through, but she gave no clues as to how she accomplished that.

No doubt there was solid science there, but she failed to see the subtle demonic deceptions, the twisting's and undermining's of the demons. That's what the demon's do! They were present there, diabolically influencing and distorting at every chance. For example let's take a man with no impulse control, who has a family history of diabetes. No impulse control can be symptomatic of demonic oppression. It's the polar opposite of the biblically correct attitude of self-discipline. The demons could build an emotional "hot button," or one may be present as the result of inequities. Whatever the source, the use of that "hot button" drove compulsions leading to the purchase of surgery drinks, salty snacks. And to numerous restaurant meals, and anything highly processed, anything out of a package or a box. As the gentleman aged, he would start crashing after meals, strange, what could that be about? How about type II diabetes or heart disease; and that's how they operate.

As for schizophrenia, some people beat it on their own. Like the people whose lifestyle corresponds to Godly principles, and who know how too tenaciously resist and undercut the demonic exploits aimed at them, and keeping at it. Being committed

and determined that is, some can eventually recover. Some peo-
ple encounter schizophrenia in the natural. And in this day and
age with the Lord coming soon, I cannot believe that the demons
would miss any opportunity to injure, and I'd bet they're there
too. It's certainly worth checking out! Do a Google search, and
you'll find "that hearing voices" is now a new "normal" for many
people. The influence of Lucifer's minions in our world expands
exponentially, through the misinformed and unbelieving and
then into the church. It's supposed to be the church that under-
stands, and then helps its own despite the world's systems. Not
the other way around, they so often have it all wrong. And it's
not like the secular doctors have a choice either; they must treat
the results of the demonic, the damages that are done, as they
cannot address the spiritual root causes.

After I'd vacationed and had some recovery time with my
friend Rob Joy in Fort Collins, Colorado. I took a flight to meet up with
the Anastasis in a West African port. Mercy Ships was clearly a mixed
bag; the work could be great, but as usual I was an odd duck. There
weren't many people my age to socialize with, and most of the crewmembers had families aboard, and so it was often a lonely place for
me to be. There was a sizable library aboard, and during my seven
years there, I read everything of any interest no matter how remote, as
well as adding to the collection. Reading and discussions in the evenings were what drew my interest. Often there were folks about relaxing somewhere, folks with which to speak. These were conversations
with special people, as the crew was entirely volunteers from twenty
five or so, different nations, and every background and culture I could
imagine. But sometimes there just was no one about, and it was pretty
lonely. There weren't many others in the same boat as I, so to speak,
it's just the way it was and I was reconciled to it accustomed to it. You
see I had an idea of just how screwed up I might be, I just didn't know
the source of it all. I remember an event that took place when I lived
in Colorado Springs, Colorado. I had gone for a walk and was a block
from the house when I noticed an open-top jeep coming up the street.
The driver was a morbidly obese, downtrodden looking guy, and sitting next to him was another miserable looking specimen, I'd guess his
wife.

In the back, there were three butter-ball kids, and the whole crew looked utterly miserable! I thought then, "Some people shouldn't have children." "They should show a bit of character and stop the misery at their doorsteps." And so, I made a silent vow not to have a family. I figured that screwed up as I was any family I attempted would have to be a disaster. So I just wouldn't go there. That attitude stuck; it became a part of my thinking and emotions, and if any gal showed interest in me. If they didn't back off I would. I paid a high price for that vow. I'm old and all alone now. But I remain convinced that it was the best thing for me to have done, especially at that time. Now, today, it's irrelevant. And that was long before I'd gotten saved. Back then, I had no idea there was a God of new beginnings. To continue, at that time Mercy Ships had three ships, and the Anastasis was the largest. These vessels worked to support the local churches in the ports they visited. The Anastasis was to specialize in head/neck, and facial surgeries that had short recovery times and huge impacts for the patients. The ministry was there to bless in any way it could from delivering supplies and medications to constructing local clinics and helping as opportunity allowed.

After six years on the M/V Anastasis I was asked to take on a prosthetics project for Mercy Ships. It looked like the Lord had intended it just for me. The CEO Simonne Dyer, asked me to pray and think about the proposal. Later, after a confirming scripture arrived in my heart. I started a search for a replacement tech for the dental/facial prosthetics lab. It bore fruit, a Welsh couple asked to join as crew on the ship, and the gal had a degree from a Welsh University in Dental Laboratory Prosthetics. Over the summer and fall seasons I stayed in touch with them. Then at last, Carolyn and her husband arrived. They were personable, gentle folks, but I quickly realized that Carolyn had only prepared for "production" laboratory work; she didn't know much. The "specialty labs" like I had, did high quality, close tolerance work a different ball game. This type of work was a lot more expensive and involved for the dentist, but it can withstand the test of time. Over time, "production" work is deeply flawed. So I had her work duties assigned to me for the five month DTS to try to train her.

But I later wondered if my efforts were worthwhile; she just wouldn't engage, it was like she didn't really want to be there, maybe it was me? The reason I tell you this is to keep my story accurate, and this is what occurred. But, more than that, I wanted to share that I cannot understand this type of behavior. Why should people fail to engage? It's a mystery to me. In dealing with the demonic, you must, you unequivocally MUST, fight and cast them out. You cannot appease them; you cannot medicate them out, and you cannot therapeutically remove them. They must be cast out, engaged and defeated with the authority of the Lord Jesus Christ. Accept no substitutes. And so, off to the races. I packed my belongings and left the lab behind, the place that contained all of my equipment and supplies. Carolyn had added a bit to the equipment and stayed for a while. She had blessed some folks. And after the labs construction I had provided and procured enough tools and supplies that a skilled tech could make about anything, especially anything facial or intra-oral. I left a complete setup in place, and I still feel good about that. A couple of flights later my plane arrived in the Dallas Texas airport, and from there I checked into Mercy Ship's Headquarters in Garden Valley, Texas.

I was following the direction I'd received from the Lord while on the ship as best as I could. I believe the Apostle Paul would call this move being obedient to my heavenly vision; that's cool. That's a good way to live. This is what was going on: the proposal Mercy Ships CEO. Simonne Dyer offered me. Had to do with an evaluation for Global Marine Inc., an offshore oil exploration company. I was asked to evaluate a low-tech, but very useful method of making artificial lower limbs, developed in Jaipur, India. Global Marine was exploring having Mercy Ships adapt this Indian technique for building "below-the-knee" lower limbs as a project they'd sponsor. The results of my research indicated that this was a splendid system indeed, especially for India. Other cultures, however, viewed it as too low tech for them. I also evaluated how lower limbs were being made in the States. I visited local area businesses that produced lower limbs, talked with the owners and the techs, and got an idea of the techniques and costs involved. After visiting several cities, and on the last stop. I discovered a new system, designed by Seattle Prosthetics Research Institute.

This system utilized computer-aided-design and computer aided manufacturing processes, named the M+IND, lower-limb-building system. After a successful evaluation, it was picked up by the U.S. Department of Veterans Affairs for use in their Hospital Systems. I wrote a full report on the trip and recommended the M+IND System to the Medical Department; they decided that this was the system that had the greatest appeal and had the best cost to benefits. They suggested that Mercy Ships should take up this project as Global Marine had, in the meantime, reconsidered it. I was then asked to do it. First off, I had to introduce the venture to Mercy Ships Board for their approval. The board members were interested in the project but leery of the expense. I explained that I would do the fund raising. But, I interjected; I would not do the project on the cheap.

I explained further that I would procure only premium quality items, and make sure that all purchases would be of high quality and industrial strength. I asked the board to allow me to get the "best products at the most reasonable price," or I would not do it, and they agreed. I think Don Stephens, the founder of Mercy Ships was the driving force behind the project, and I was told to go do it. I was exercising a principle here. Maybe you've seen those ads for donated services to emerging nations. Like the one where the local guy is proudly showing off his new eyeglasses, "Our new friend loves his new glasses that you kindly provided, and at only $3.00 a pair." Well, would you want a pair of $3.00 frames? I doubt it. When you give a poor person something it had better be rugged, reliable, and made from quality materials as they will see no maintenance and the recipient has no options when it breaks. Sorry for the sermon, but that's an example of how I've tried to reason these things out, in this Christian walk. I love serving the Lord and working in the Kingdom with His people. I want to make a proper job of it.

"Looking back, an Overview"

≈≈≈

*My season in the Discipleship Training School on the M/V Ana-
stasis that started my time in missions, proved to be a turning
point in my life. Not because it provided all needed direction, education and spiritual equipping. But because it was a fresh
start, and it gave me an improved Godly foundation. Without
that foundation I wouldn't have done as well as I did in Mercy
Ships. That Godly foundation was a bulwark and point of resistance to my spiritual enemies as all true Christian teaching
should be. It's what we accomplish when we flesh out and live
by those Christian teachings, which will determine a chunk of
our satisfaction in life. It's easy just doing the "expected" work-
aday functions. But, when you're working for others and doing
it in the "upside down" to this world's systems, "prefer one another" manner of Jesus Christ. You'll soon realize this; that it's
not an easy or comfortable habit for one to acquire; it's hard.
Yet it's something we must work at, hoping to achieve. It's not
easy; it's Godly.*

"Thoughts to take Away"

≈≈≈

*When you do your work for the Kingdom, please consider the
quality of what you do and try not to leave things undone.
Then, when we pause to consider the "Grace of God" in our
lives, remember, it's not just about "our sins." It's equally, about
our "righteousness" and how it's as dirty rags to Christ.*

Chapter-Six

- Operation Sea Legs -

So, "once more unto the breach, dear friends, once more!" I was now the occupant of a well experienced desk, in the medical department's office spaces in Mercy Ships "Administrative and Executive Building." It was pretty high cotton for a boy from Brooklyn, N.Y., a self-educated rather blunt one at that. One of the best things about Mercy Ships, in the offices or on the ships was the high caliber of people that were volunteering. I genuinely admired many of them and had a lot of respect for the leadership. These were people whose best wishes were to live a life of value, serving and following the Lord. Cool, a lifestyle and heart condition that was the exact opposite of a biker! I had thought it through and considered it a small loss to leave behind all my dental lab equipment and supplies. Doing this for the privilege of doing what I was supposed to do - wholeheartedly repent of my sins, and follow the Lord when and where He leads. I had that much right. First off, I had to decide on what to do with this prosthetics project, and how to go about that. So I put together an overall project plan and outline. Then, I had to find someone who was an expert in this prosthetics arena, someone who was available and willing to help. And, to get the project started off on the right foot, it was going to need funding! On reflection, I thought I should take a course in "grant writing," and there was one at the Dallas Public Library. A curious thing happened on the course's last day. My "Operation Sea Legs" proposal was presented for evaluation by the class. The instructor loved the all-volunteer, non-salaried aspect of Mercy Ships, and the proposal was read. The whole class got stuck on a sentence in the opening statement. They were stuck trying to decide if I'd crafted a complete sentence, or not, and I didn't know. I hadn't written as much as a long letter in twenty years. So, my time was used up in an English debate, sigh. Lesson learned - find editors, relearn written English, sigh.

The prosthetics project had been named "Operation Sea Legs," by Mercy Ships President, Don Stephens, which, unfortunately, didn't translate so well. So it was renamed "New Steps," sometime later. One of the things I most valued from that project was that it gave me a chance to leave an enduring legacy in Mercy Ships. You see I was the first person to attempt "grant writing" and to succeed at it. And regarding the organization some years later, when procurement became much easier and professional grant writers replaced me, was quite satisfying. I helped blazed that trail, and it turned out to be a five year journey.

Through friends in Fort Collins, Colorado, I met Richard, a Prosthetist who was to help me develop the Prosthetics lab. This was a bit later when the container was located on the grounds outback, hard by the maintenance shed. That lab was to be a new, lightweight, all-aluminum and specially built, 10' by 8' by 40' "High-cube" shipping-container. The standard (and quite heavy) steel shipping container, was 8' by 8' by 40' and felt so small when in it – that it was claustrophobic. A "high-cube," like the one I found was much better. This one was a beauty; it had been an experiment that was fabricated by its builder as a new approach to shipping frozen products. The design looked impressive on paper but failed in practice, and we got the container at a good price, with the improved flooring and walls still intact. We found the container through an advert in a shipping magazine. A Christian man had placed it, and when I called for information he was curious about who and what Mercy Ships was. The way this all came together was through a med student working on a grad project as an intern. We provided him a place to work, a phone, and an internet connection right next to me. And as we talked about his projects and concerns he taught me something. This was, that he could get almost any information he needed to in just seven phone calls. If you explained yourself as someone needing help and qualified to use it. People wanted to help and do it effectively. That knowledge was to serve me well. I drove to Jacksonville Florida, saw the container amongst a half dozen others and bought it with funds from a grant from the Chatlos Foundation. An exceptional family foundation that wanted to help establish the prosthetics project. The forty foot aluminum container was shiny, bright white, and looked great. As part of the deal we had a local fabrication shop do some additional work on the back and inside the container.

Then shipped it to the offices in Texas, as parts like the work-benches, storage racks, and equipment arrived. They'd go into storage in the maintenance shed until needed, and I'd spend my mornings working inside the container. I'd work hard, starting early and staying at it until it just got too darned hot. Then, I'd transition into the highly anticipated air-conditioning of the offices, working on the grant re-searching and writing, and later, reporting and planning for the rest of the day. Sea Legs was a pretty small project, but plenty for one per-son. We designed the container to hold a prosthetist, his tech, and all other activities elsewhere. There would be a team on deployment, but the container was a workspace and patient exam area.

I wonder these days, how difficult it might have been working with me, back then. Our diabolical enemy, being the en-emy that he is with his so subtle manipulation of our emotions. Makes for some challenging and awkward people. I knew I was stressed, what with anxiously waiting on funding appeals, and highly valued equipment sometimes astray, or sometimes long overdue. I was also in an unusual position. I was one of the few non-medical and non-university educated persons in the depart-ment, and the administration kept putting different people over me. However, I was still doing the daily work and decision mak-ing. I'd ask for input at various stages and was ready to comply, but I was still "the chief cook and bottle washer," and that didn't sit so well with some others. It was often a damned if you do and damned if you don't, sort of situation. They were the profession-als and their opinions were supposed to count. But I had the task of making it all work. Sometimes, I had to ignore their directions and advice, and sometimes I'd wish I'd followed it, just a tight place. Some of that problem set was entirely of my own creation although I couldn't see it, not back then. (Remember that analogy of the finger over the garden hose nozzle?). And few people had a clear picture of what I was building. It was just gradually, get-ting done. My usual pace was at a run - and on thinking back on those days this question presents itself. Could it possibly be that demonic oppression laced through my thoughts and emotions? There was plenty of ammunition for them from the continual pres-sure to accomplish things. Firstly, as things needed doing, and I often had no practical support that was genuinely helpful. Other times there were folks helping, quite a lot, but it was still, a strange spot altogether.

• [Forgive this intrusion into the story.] While typing away on my laptop, trying to remember those days and the way I felt back then. I realized I felt quite anxious and stressed. I stopped everything, took a short walk and came back to pray. **"Lord Jesus Christ, please intercede between me and those demonic spirits outside me, ones working to produce this stress and anxiety and destroy them all." Thanks, Lord. Amen.**

• Immediately, I felt at peace and thought about the pleasure of walking with the Lord to the consternation of our enemies. One's we all face - thanks again Lord! This book does gets its resistance! Sometimes in life we get picked on, it's not a real big deal right now. Just life.

• Overall, we are held accountable for defeating our inward spiritual enemies, those demonic trespassers and attackers. Once achieved, the Lord is right there, ready when called in intercessory prayer and prepared to destroy those enemies in free circulation and other areas. Places outside of us, in His arena, sending the attacking spirits off to the pit. Those evil spirits sent my way, (by upper management,) prodding and testing, working against me, and always seeking opportunities to do me mischief, and often-times, to block this book.

Offhand, I'd say that demonic attack provided the correct answer to my question, in the paragraph above this bulleted sequence!
Yup-er...

In addition to the Colorado Springs CO. prosthetist helping with the design of the prosthetics lab, I was fortunate to have had the help of some professional electricians. Occasionally, I'd recruit someone to help with things I had no knowledge of, like water and vacuum systems, that was a biggie; thanks, Tom Vel. But, often, it was the suppliers and tech support people answering questions, and just plain head scratching, try again if something went a kilter, style of construction. Towards the end of the construction phase, I was tasked with recruiting an experienced prosthetist. And similar to the development of the dental lab on the ship.

When I needed help, I started asking whoever. Just anyone who I thought might be able to help. I'd start out by looking at trade magazines, the local phone book and the Internet for contacts. And just like back on the Anastasis', as I'd engaged and was already working on the project, others would join in and together we'd get it built. But, had I dropped it on someone else's desk, it would have gone to the bottom of the stack. So pretty soon, I was phoning about, casting around and energetically searching, looking for a Prosthetist to use the MIN+D CAD-CAM System. Originally, it was thought I'd go to Seattle Washington, for training by Seattle's Prosthetics Research Studio. But, there was no one to take on my lab building chores. So I was stuck searching for a prosthetist, and I found this man through the seven calls teaching. Which I was to learn has a definite downside! Let's call him Larry Harry Led. In checking his references red flags were out, he didn't seem to stick to things. I knew an orthopedist that worked with Mercy Ships, and was acquainted with him. He said he seemed to be doing well in Northern Colorado, where he had a business making and fitting prosthetic limbs. Until one day, he just disappeared and left his patients and clients hanging.

That was scary, but sometimes in this volunteer world you needed to go with whoever's available, and he was the only one with the necessary skills I could find. Larry was a university trained prosthetist. He could make orthotic appliances and lower limbs, above or below the knee. And above the knee prosthetics can be remarkably difficult, so he had exceptional skills. Besides that, I knew that the Lord had given me such an incredible break in my salvation and conversion. And maybe, just maybe, Larry would prove to be a suitable candidate for passing that on. In conversations with him, I heard no indications he actually was a Christian man. Larry and I, we continued our phone conversations, and then Larry unexpectedly came to Texas and arrived at the base. He said hello, and disappeared; what the? I couldn't believe this. But he said later, he had to walk around on his own and talk to folks, seeing what he needed to. It was kind of strange behavior. Then he just up and left without a word more to me, weird. Much to my surprise! Larry showed up for the next DTS. "So maybe this is going to be OK" was my thought then.

A Spiritual Warfare Ensemble

The Discipleship Training School on the base was an entity all of its own, they worked with their departmental resources and staffing. The students and the Mercy Ships staff ate meals together; they did mission related activities, and students were sometimes guests in staffer's homes. But they were quite distinct from each other in their work functions, as it should be. There was little social overlap, but still, making friendships and developing working relationships was pretty standard stuff. Mercy Ships and YWAM, the parent groups are Christian Missionary organizations and all volunteer (at that time in Mercy Ships) and non-salaried. You were required to raise your personal support, and being short of cash and understaffed was about average then. This non-salaried volunteering most often worked like this. Those with extended families and many friends or wealthy in-laws lived a fairly standard, lower middle class, North American lifestyle. Those from smaller families, who had sold a home or business or retired early, often struggled. Individual fund raising remains a highly problematic arena! I was amongst the latter, but people learned to get along and work together.

But not Larry, the guy barely had two words for me or anyone else. During his DTS, I learned that while he didn't do anything wrong, he just didn't do anything right. He didn't provide a reason for the administration to dismiss him, he just wasn't a regular part of the course. He wasn't a part of anything, and he even slept outside in a hammock! When I asked the leadership how he was doing, they gave me little encouragement. Each class was different, and some were better than others. In most classes, there were those students who didn't seem to get seriously involved with the subjects or the speakers. Some of these students returned later, when they'd digested things, and had remarkably changed as people. Hopefully, Larry was going to be one of those. After the class outreach, Larry returned to join the Sea Legs staff, and he didn't seem to think much of the project. He'd stand there watching me work and offer little help or assistance. But, sometimes, sometimes he was OK, and I'd get his participation; I never knew. I arranged for special training for him, flying him to Detroit, Michigan, to learn the CAD/CAM prosthetic software program.

The MIN+D system and equipment with the Apple computers and CAD/CAM digitizing tools and Larry did poorly. He showed up but didn't engage, again. Oh no, groan, not another Carolyn. Eventually deployment time arrived, and we left on outreach to Leon, Nicaragua. To the only hospital that wasn't under the thumb of the local communist committees and with whom Mercy Ships and I had a close relationship. We were going there to make (below-the-knee) lower limbs for those people who had lost theirs to landmines. This project was to be a showcase for the MIN+D prosthetic system in the Americas. We hoped that this would be developed further, on an even larger scale mutating into affordable local treatment for those needing lower limbs. Similar styles of lower limbs sold in the US for about $5,000., at that time, and we were building them for $400. These legs were free for anyone needing them. The only condition was that the patient would complete the training from the hospital's physical therapists, training that would physically prepare them to wear a prosthesis. The hospital's therapists had a list of these patients they'd prepared for us. Come one, come all. Once again, things didn't go as planned.

Leon's, "Electrical Power Company" hooked up the three-phase electrical power from the pole to the container wrong. And at first I didn't realize this, I'm not an electrician, and I'd needed the help of electricians to design and build the thing, and was soon out of my element. Essentially, electrical things didn't work properly. Finally, the city got the power corrected, and I got the CAD/CAM equipment operating. Then, Larry needed differing things. For example, we hadn't been allowed to ship solvents in the container itself, and they were really hard to find locally. Eventually he got what he wanted. OK fine. Larry had gotten his wishes, and then he made it clear he was in charge and I had no business there. I learned some time later that he'd bullied the hospital's staff people who came to the container. He'd also damaged the relationships I'd built with the hospital administrator and surgeons over the preceding two years. After all this work, Sea Legs was going downhill fast. I know life's not fair, but why was this so hard? Then, the man deserted his tasks and went to the beach drinking, staying at it until some staffers from the hospital found him and brought him back.

41

While Larry went AWOL a short-term volunteer, a prosthetist from North Carolina flew down. He and I worked late all week to get Larry's backlog of limbs done, and the MIN+D system worked quite well; I was really pleased. I thoroughly enjoyed working with this man, it was fun building the legs, and I got to be a prosthetist techie for a little bit. Then Larry showed up and declared that since all the work was up to date, a holiday was in order!

Mercy Ships heard about these difficulties long distance and sent a man down to see what was what. Curtis had originally been in charge of the "Sea Legs" project and had stepped down as he had no knowledge of all the processes, or the time to learn them. Curtis was an honest, affable, soft-spoken kind man and a hard worker, but he was not an analyst. He talked with project folks and closeted with Larry and told me it was my fault. Larry was the professional, and everything was fine, just fine if I just went along with him. I'd seen this before; one of the great strengths of Mercy Ships was the volunteer nature of the staff. It was also one of its greatest weaknesses. Having a head full of training and varying degrees was an excellent draw. But it all goes south, if the head full of training was twisted and the heart was wrong, and that was happening here. Me, I was just a tech who could make lots of useful things and make them well. An associate's degree as a dental laboratory tech didn't cut it, not amongst some of the folks with significant investments in their educations. So I said fine, just let me out of there and I got so sick I almost died. For some months, I'd been sickly and struggling along, and things kept getting worse. Larry was upset; he needed me fetching things for him! Several weeks later I got my chance to escape and left there, pronto. A few days before leaving I had looked in the mirror, and my eyes and lips were black, I was that close to death. I was lucky that one of the project's team was a retired nurse, and she kept feeding me things to keep my electrolytes from getting completely out of whack. I got to the airport and on the plane, and didn't look back. The first leg of my flight was back to Lindale Texas, and then, off to visit friends in Fort Collins, Colorado, for a few months of rest and rebuilding. Oddly enough, getting back to Western food and tasty, Tex-Mex cuisine, cured my condition temporally, but it took years to discover and rid myself of all the parasites.

Meanwhile, the project struggled along for the next six months, putting out about half the production it'd been designed for. As Larry failed to keep the MIN+D equipment going or to use it properly. Some folks aren't adept with complex tools, and that seemed to be the case here. Larry would screw the computers up, misuse the prosthetics program and walk away and do things by hand. So it was mostly a disaster, and eventually Mercy Ships sent the senior staff counselor to the project in Leon to spend a week and try to figure out what to do. I had submitted a report on my return on what had been going on and that report went unheeded. When the counselor returned, he backed up what I'd said; the project came to a halt, and Larry was fired. In my fourteen years with Mercy Ships, I knew of only a handful out of thousands who volunteered that were fired, that's not what the organization was about. It was all about restoring relationships; connections between God and us and people to people, firing someone was a rare and drastic action.

On thinking back to those days, this event was terribly sad. Here was a life without Jesus and with a twisted heart. Some people just don't stand a chance, and that's Larry. Then I met an orthopedist who knew him, he and the counselor said he was a betrayer, a controller and manipulator, a sick man. (They got to know him well enough, but I hadn't.) Larry didn't let me get close enough to understand him and now I know why. The Lord showed me in a dream one night that Larry had suffered abuse as a child, and all his emotions were rooted in demonic strongholds. At a project debriefing, put on by the counseling staff some months later; the lead counselor explicitly stated the emotional problems Larry had displayed. He sat there acknowledging and nodding his head; he knew his condition. That's why he'd hid out and snuck through his DTS. What a waste! This man had every opportunity while he was with the mission to get to know the Lord and work on his problems.

But, the demons are highly skilled. Through it all, I learned a favorite tactic of theirs. The demons in one person co-operate with the demons in another person setting them at odds. They wreck relationships, prevent friendships, make individuals isolated and bring couples to conflict. And they're quite skilled at it. That's what was happening here, Larry was a spoiler! I prayed long and hard for this guy's salvation it was the only way I could be sure I'd forgiven him. He sure gave me a hard time. I hope he comes to the knowledge of God, to redemption and to salvation. I don't have to be mad at him or even think back on him. I wish him the best. I also know this, those people the demons use they also destroy. That's what they do: steal and kill and destroy. And those (useful idiots) like Larry, whom they use to help them in their demonic missions they especially despise. It's similar to how a con-man might hate his mark, his victim being swindled and his dupe. And what about the blasted demons, what's up with them? I once read a description somewhere, which fits them well and is supported by my experiences. They're fallen angels, driven insane by their ceaseless cruelties. Please realize this, one of the principal things that saves us from their designs altogether, is that the power of the wicked intentions they plan towards us fails to be matched by their abilities. Sometimes they are just plain stupid, and always, they are the trash of the spiritual universe! And as trash, they're only fit for the fire. Demons are dangerous when well concealed, when it's not realized that they're about. And an irritating troublesomeness when detected, and need to be dealt with, promptly. Typically they're just subtle, negative, destructive, background noise, it's up to you. You must decide whether to deal with them or not.

"Looking back, an Overview"

≈≈≈

I found it hard to accept that the Lord had saddled me with Larry. When I asked Him why, I heard a reply deep in my soul, "because I knew you could take it." One day, I've just got to ask Him about that. For now, I just know that God is Sovereign, He can do whatever He chooses, when He chooses, as He chooses.

"Thoughts to take Away"

≈≈≈

It's easy to forget: "His ways are higher than our ways."

Chapter-Seven

- What a way to take a Trip -

W hile I recovered my health with Rob Joy in Fort Collins, CO. I called the computer department at Mercy Ships headquarters. The network back then was UNIX based at the server level and Microsoft for the desktops and was right on the cutting edge. I inquired if they could get any use out of an Apple-Mac user and a new Microsoft practitioner of those systems. Kelvin, who was in charge of the (IT) information department said, yes sure, come and learn so I did. My reasoning was: yes, I could make pretty decent facial parts, the artificial eyes and facial prosthetics. But I couldn't start a business, not without spending years training to meet state licensing; I was self-taught. I could also do dental lab work again, but I didn't want to. Time had moved on, and now twelve years later, states required licensing for ownership or you couldn't bill the dentists. Mostly, I just didn't want to start working at the bottom again, not in my old disciplines not again. So, on to computers at Mercy Ships those things were beginning to get useful.

I thought I was still young enough to get hired in computers, especially with in demand skills. Maybe even make a decent living, and without having to start my own business again; I'd had enough with eighty hour weeks. So, I showed up and started working with PC's and taking "Microsoft Certified Systems Engineering" courses. Eventually, I earned five MS Certifications, striving to understand the computer/server systems. It was excellent training. I enjoyed computer department projects at Mercy Ships, like lightning proofing the computer room and the telephone systems. That was engaging and hard work. The Mercy Ships' Garden Valley property was in "Tornado Alley." A good amount of all the trees had bark missing from lightning strikes. It was a difficult site for computer networks and phone systems. I also helped upgrade computers and tried to help users with their applications - a fruitless job. Too many users just wanted to be shown instant cures for their headaches. Getting quick fixes without devoting any time or effort on your own doesn't work so well.

When you fix stuff yourself, you remember! Why couldn't they buy a book and use it? The few that did, they were good to work with; rant over. Some users complained that IT folks made them feel stupid. And there was some justification for that. And some individuals from IT were also frustrated, especially with users who wanted to utilize the full features of word processors and other powerful applications, without having practiced on or studied them. Once again, it was the volunteer nature of the staffing that was at the heart of the matter. And it was about time for me to take a break. If I didn't, I'd have no Social Security retirement benefits. The main thing from my two years in the computer department was that I'd gotten some IT experience, and that's hard to get starting out. I felt I'd learned enough about PC's and networking to find employment. And as I was packing and preparing to depart Mercy Ships, I happened to leave my apartment and glanced to the road to see Don Stephens in his pickup coming to the curb. It was quite nice of Don, taking a chance to come by to say good-bye. Over the years, Don was an example of integrity and resourcefulness to me. As I said earlier, I was proud to have served under him.

It's funny; I've been mentioned in three books. Two were by Don, and I've been amused by the wrong dates, etc., and now, here I am writing this and trying hard to keep it all straight. Well, it's not so easy my writing this book, and this is my best effort so far and it seems quite close to me. I've worked hard to ensure a revealing effort, working to confound the demonic letting in as much light on this subject as I can. I'm doing this in the hope that when you reach the books concluding (Pastor Jenkins Deliverance Script) segment, which contains a practical, repeatable, measurable method of combating the demonic. (The best I've found). You'll want to use it. And what I've attempted to illustrate in both of these books, and most especially Book Two. Is that during the full-blown demonic oppression that I experienced, I eventually found myself getting deeply, earnestly, into the minutiae of my life. All of it - even into my family's long history. Our spiritual enemies use unresolved familial - spiritual issues to the fullest degree, against us, and these issues must reach a conclusion. The only way is through spiritual means, and my story outlines a proven, workable way, of helping obtain full sanctification from the demonic. Because, the Holy Spirit will take you places you couldn't find otherwise, except when you are under attack as I was. Or, in a significantly better approach, (Oh yes, please Lord,) by becoming deeply involved in your personal sanctification. By your free choice. And similarly, through methods such as these. Either way, you'll want to get close and see clearly, and only He can work with you, getting you to the issues deepest roots. So, it's like seeing your life's events, under high magnification enabled by the Holy Spirit. Realizing the consequences and the actualities of any sin and defining those issues, and you can't do it without Him. As I write this now after being fully freed from the demonic. I'm viewing these same roots, from a clearer "long-range view." I'm striving to keep it all organized and working hard to provide an overview of my life's lessons. I'm doing this so you can see how these things worked, and hopefully, benefit from my misery, suffering, and the ultimate success. That victory kindly provided by the Holy Spirit and just plain hard work.

OK, I piled my belongings into a U-Haul and off to Fort Collins to stay with Rob and get back to work. Fourteen years in missions is hard on the pocketbook and trying to live on the cheap is hard on the soul. Compensated work was required. After arriving at the house, I was grateful for a friend and a place to start over. I delighted in my new life in my new home in Colorado. I set up a computer and began a job search and did all the usual things people do after a move. Temporary jobs were what I found, and some were engaging like doing network upgrades for Hewett-Packard or just helping small businesses. They worked for the meantime and kept me alive. It wasn't so easy then, not like it used to be when I was younger and looked for work. I was fifty four, and it took a few months until I found a job with a local employer, through Rob. I'll call these guys "Home Professionals." My job was fairly straightforward; I had to keep my boss, Freddy, out of the server room. Like lots of simple sounding tasks, it was complex in its components. Overall, the job was to develop company email from a number of old fashioned dial-up accounts to an up to date system. To do that, I needed to get the servers running properly. After accomplishing that I went on to install a Microsoft Exchange, E-mail Server, which dramatically improved their e-mail services. I setup networked application backups and worked to protect the network from hackers and to improve the Internet access, which was the foundation of the business.

And above all, I kept Freddy out of the server room. At the offices of Home Professionals, there was a small IT department with a minor genius programmer, named Harvey, and a large Microsoft SQL Server Database. There was also a bunch of different desktop computers in various conditions. It was a pretty decent place to start out at, as Freddy was more of a politician than an IT administrator, and that was to my advantage. I began by doing the research to figure out how to achieve the departmental goals; that is without getting burnt from too many mistakes. Thankfully, Freddy understood this took many long hours and was going to be slow to implement as lots of out of date things needed to be upgraded. I got lucky with the mistakes and managed to get some useful things accomplished quickly. The work went forward, and the only real problems I had were with the users on the network. Home Professionals was a bit of a schlock outfit. They claimed to be a fantastic place to work, and even took out adverts in the paper stating that.

They talked like a large family but paid the lowest wages possible with minimal health care. I think what they really wanted was a family of coolies, glued to their desks. And they weren't shy, not at all, not about laying off the highest paid hourly wage earners whenever sales slowed, indicating to them that it was time to protect the company officers generous paychecks. Trying to keep users happy with low-performance computers, and poorly paid and unhappy people doesn't work so well. I almost solved that problem by designing and selling to the company, a plan to add a call-center to the network. The call-center had modern terminals that I could remotely administer from the server room, aha, out of the line of fire as the call center had its manager for its disgruntled employees. So that set of politics was soon out of my hair. But I still had to put up with unhappy people, and that got sticky. I did notice that, the unhappier a person was, the more difficult and demanding they were as a network user; it was not a healthy recipe. Eventually, I had enough of this outfit, quit the company, and started doing part-time small business consulting. There are outstanding wages as a consultant; the problem was getting enough hours. Freddy started hiring me back as a consultant, and the money was lots better.

And they'd also hired a full-time computer support guy. It was good that I was working a part-time job as I experienced my first bout of heart trouble. It was strange; I would run out of energy, quickly. And I had chest pain on exertion, and I didn't do so well in the blustery Colorado winter. Fortunately, I still had health insurance, and I managed to survive long enough to get a stent implanted to open up a blocked artery, fending off a full-blown heart attack. This stent was supposed to restore full blood flow to the heart, but something strange was going on. My arms would tingle and ache, right at the pressure points. I'd ask my cardio doctor what that was about, and he had no explanation. I'd ask my health care provider and get no answer. So, I'd spend hours on the Internet investigating supplements, diet and weight loss. And I figured I just had to keep briskly walking while I tried to figure out what supplements and exercise limits were going to help me. Sometimes I got significant benefits from all the supplements, sometimes not. Incidentally the best supplement I've found altogether, is known as MSM, Organic Sulphur, its outstanding.

I didn't have a clue then, but the symptoms the medical folks couldn't identify for me weren't just unusual health issues. After all, I'd led a fairly colorful life. Demonic attacks can so mimic physical symptoms, heart attacks and such, that people you consult with will have no answers for you. But you, you're still stuck, you're still swamped with the pain and the physical effects. Unfortunately, attending church and being involved in the body of Christ was of no benefit either, It's as though anything spiritual that didn't involve raising your hands and feeling good was off the radar. Demonic oppression was a strange and unmentioned problem. It's such an overlooked, avoided topic that it's difficult to get the information you need, in most churches anyway. It was especially hard to understand how demons might affect a person physically; this wasn't a question to be introduced, not anytime, and it seemed to be of no significance. I've noticed though that parishioners do get sick and diseased, and few understand what to do. Clearly, Doctors have their limits bless them for trying. I still don't understand; Jesus devoted about one third of his ministry to deliverance and healing, and deliverance quite often is physically healing, expect it. Why then, is this not a topic for the bulletin board at church? Why, after twenty three years of church going and mission's activities, why couldn't I remember hearing anything of this at any church I regularly attended, at any time? That is before my "days of trouble" styled demonic oppression began? It doesn't have to be a full blast exposure as I'm attempting. But how about a "Bondage Breaker" "authored by Neil Anderson," deliverance conference? I attended one at a church in Loveland a neighboring town, and it was straightforward and useful; no problem. Just not an in-depth assault on the enemy like the concluding script offered in this book, sigh.

The next few years were a time of trying to get in shape physically, which included hours and more hours of power walking, exercises and diet. And it didn't do much good. It seemed as though there were limits to what I could achieve then. Spiritually, it was time for visiting different churches in Fort Collins and Loveland. At one church in Loveland, I met a gal from my old Anastasis DTS at a small group meeting. Lisa and I touched bases, and it happened that she liked my friend Rob. They dated for quite a while and eventually grow to care for each other. Finally with a job move to Texas, Rob and Lisa got hitched. When Rob and Lisa moved to Texas, I rented an apartment, furnished it, and it was quite comfortable. By this time at Home Professionals, I'd accepted full time work again, and at an entirely competitive wage, yes! The network I had improved over all my earlier times there, was now connected by leased lines to three other locations which worked to centralize email and data storage and had become obsolete. So, I built a more advanced system running alongside the existing one, and got ready to swap them over. But users were still the main problem, and I was fed up with the bad attitudes. Altogether I'd had enough of Home Professionals. And then, I learned that they wanted to replace my position with a new one, a programmer/administrator, (I'm not a programmer) so an upcoming layoff looked pretty spiffy to me. Over a long weekend, we switched to the new system, and I walked out breathing a sigh of relief. No more rubbish from those disgruntled users! Now it was time to fight for better health, physically and spiritually. The physical side plateaued relatively soon. It seemed I could only get so far in my quest to get in good condition? Continuing on, after a long search and a season of visiting area churches, I'd found a new church.

New Hope Fellowship, this was a place that needed folks, it was small, and almost all the parishioners were related. And after meeting the pastor, it seemed I might be able to contribute to the church. Also, happily, I'd gotten a new and excellent job at an architectural consultancy! But the best thing from my time then was this: I'd decided to try reading the Word from a different perspective looking to see what it would say to me. I did it by disregarding the formatting (chapters & verse numbers, notes etc.) and read it as I would a long letter. On reflecting on all the hours spent reading on the Anastasis and listening to the twice weekly afternoon speakers, I remembered this event. Once, a guest worship leader came to the Anastasis intending to bless us. He came equipped with a keyboard and sound system, and he recited the entire book of Romans and played the keyboard along with it, it was gorgeous. I wanted some more of that – "that quoted aloud style," just for me. When I was a new Christian, I'd been persuaded to read the Bible while analyzing it for content and interpreting it for contemporary meaning; that was how it was to be read. Or was it? For some time then, there had been an "inaudible voice" a critical attitude. One which was intruding into my reading and thoughts. An odd feeling, experienced more emotionally rather than heard in the mind, and it was speaking dissatisfaction with my Christian experience. I didn't know the source of it and wanted to be relieved of it; and I needed a way to challenge this strange feeling. Overall this looked like a valid way to see what was what. After a month at this, reading the bible very much like a letter. I just sat there one afternoon convinced in my soul, and resolved in my mind that all scripture was true; period. If I didn't understand it, fine. It still was true. If it contradicted what I had been taught, the teaching had been off. No matter what, the Bible is true, and that's it for me.

A short time later, a memorable event happened in my life. The best way I can describe it is to include the letter I wrote to my Pastor, three days later, when my head was back together.

(Please note: this letter has been edited for clarity).

A Spiritual Warfare Ensemble

Pastor Bill,

Last Wednesday morning, on September 8th, 2006, I had a remarkable experience. I recently started getting into a new book, *The Lost Art of Practicing His Presence, by James W. Goll*. It's about contemplative prayer, a manner of prayer that I'd not heard much about. And as I read that book, I gathered that I'd been praying in the very same fashion just without realizing it. I hadn't needed a name for it for practicing that form of prayer, and I felt it helped me draw closer to the Lord. Well, I don't know if what happened to me was in response to that type of prayer, that style and its intensity. But soon enough, early one morning, an amazing event occurred. I rarely dream. Often when I retire I kind of pick a daydream to relax with, as I have to think of something and eventually drift off. During the night, I usually get up a time or two. Sometimes I try sleeping somewhere else. I rarely get a truly restful night's sleep, and seldom will remember if I've dreamt, and it's rarely in color if I do. On one Wednesday morning, I slowly awoke to find myself in a kind of structure, made of translucent gold. This was incredible; this vision or was it a dream? Whatever it was, it was something markedly different, unlike anything I'd experienced any time before. This wasn't the usual half asleep, muddled, incoherent dream state. This experience was vivid, and convincing, it was so very real and immediate. The centerpiece of this dream, this vision was this massive golden structure I was in, it was an all-encompassing structure like a cavern opening into an extensive cave system. It was built entirely of translucent gold, and there were also amber and green translucent materials used in the walls, accenting the floors, pillars, and everything within this translucent and majestic mix of golden shapes. There was no obvious source of illumination; the light was just there and fully lit, all by itself. There weren't any shadows, and the light was everywhere. I was at a workbench, with mallets and chisels, plans and shavings, and was at work helping to make some part of a large, paneled, decorated door. This door, it was like something you would expect to find opening into a cathedral, like France's world famous Chartres Cathedral. That comes to mind. My workbench was in a big room like a great hall, one with pillars. Well, it was nice work, and I didn't have to be intimately concerned with its construction. As it didn't matter if I worked as hard as I could, or relaxed and enjoyed the project as it virtually put itself together. I had a role in its creation, but, it was just getting built. This panel wasn't something constructed just to match a plan; it was more of an expression of gratitude and joy in well-worked sculpture, skillfully chiseled. And it came together brilliantly. I got to thinking about where I was and looking around, I recognized that this must be some part of God's house, maybe on His Holy Mountain. Perhaps, it was one of those many mansions mentioned by Jesus? I realized then that I was feeling just like I had when I was first saved and was washed in new definitions of words. Words that I had been acquainted with before, but had little understanding of, like peace and joy. That's when I experienced real contentment for the very first time. Back then, these were all new expansive definitions. These definitions are now lodged in my heart and mind, clarified and brought into sharp focus by my salvation experience, an incredible experience some parts of which lingered with me for over a year! These were those same powerful emotions and thoughts. But now, this night, there was even more, sensations that were even more dominant and more powerful. I knew I was in a heavenly place where there was no room for sin; it just wasn't possible, it was not relevant. It was also a place where I was completely at home. I belonged there as nowhere else; it was totally encompassing and natural. I didn't want to be at home in my earthly apartment. I'd been awake and aware throughout my "vision," or "out of body experience." Whatever it was; I still don't know what it was. I do know that a good part of this was God's Kingdom in real time, and during it, towards the end. I was walking around my apartment and the apartment was the thing that was out of its place. It barely belonged there; it was somehow otherworldly. Then it was daylight, and this experience was slowly fading away, and I knew that I had to get ready for work, sadly.

I sat on the bed and gradually got myself together and with great reluctance, I pulled myself back (like using a boot strap on a boot, sigh.) Concentrating on earthly things and slipping into the necessary elements of the day. I arrived at work quite late, as this vision this heavenly trip lasted some hours. I know now that this brief life we live has a lot more certainty than before. I've been close to death while on missions, and it wasn't an overwhelming problem. Now, today, there's another aspect birthed for me. I have a new awareness resulting in my faith being even more immediate, like where I've been this night I actually belong, and that's a real comfort. I'd say I need to finish my study of *The Lost Art of Practicing His Presence* and think about what's in that book, re-read it and put it into practice. I think I've been given a taste of what might be in store for those who love the Lord, walk with Him, and work out what the Word says they should. And when we do this, this daily Christian walk. We can improve our stride by learning from those who've sojourned with the Lord, and come to new depths of intimacy, and understand deeply what it is they write about. For me, now, things are just simpler, I'm not sure why, they just are.

Paul

I still don't know why the Lord gave me that experience; I'd like more of them. Another one at this moment would be quite pleasant. It's funny; in the spiritual warfare I was to experience, so much was subjective and intangible. This vision was real. Yes- but visually and emotionally was way beyond mere reality. Reality is this stuff covering my arm, the stuff that I can pinch with my fingers. But my fingers are going away; they're going in the ground one day. Where I went that morning is someplace that I sure hope to see again. It's not going away, not ever.

"Looking back, an Overview"

≈≈≈

There are scriptures that speak of the fact that the Lord will grant us the grace and knowledge to defeat the enemy's assaults. Experience speaks of the tenacity of evil, acknowledging the persistence of our need for God to aid us in our struggles, and our sufferings, and our immediate mess. As we work to build an immediate, trusting faith in Him. Thusly, His love can conquer all, as we learn to know who we truly are in Christ Jesus.

"Thoughts to take Away"

≈≈≈

This work is about sanctification as much as anything. That place I went to in my "vision," is what sanctification prepares us for, and a place that without it you would not be prepared for.

Book-Two
A SPIRITUAL WARFARE ENSEMBLE:
Contending with- Demonic Oppression

Chapters 8 – 13

≈≈

This Sanctification Experience of mine, is the story of the all-out attacking's by the Satanic Empire to enslave or destroy me. It's a description, the illustration and reporting on the full-on spiritual warfare I endured. The sudden-onset schizophrenia, the deceptions and the victory, revealing and illuminating the weapons & tools I used to obtain that victory.

≈≈

Then, the Pastor Jenkin's: Deliverance Script, which is the locus of the story. As this is the single most useful and comprehensive tool from the arsenal I discovered and deployed, finally defeating my determined demonic enemy.

≈≈

Concluding this section, the End Notes, a listing of the resources used and available for your use and a few other well worthy offerings.

≈≈

– Bonus Sections –

Self-Deliverance Pamphlet's 101 – 201, which were an early attempt to record what worked against my entrenched enemy. Although the methods these pamphlets illustrate were unable to bring a resolution to my "time of troubles." They were helpful, and they do contain needed examples and information on self-deliverance that's hard to find elsewhere.

Just a Reminder

≈≈≈

On Avoiding Confusion:

≈≈≈

     The storyline will be justified, indented and mostly continuous and duplicates the style of writing which you've read in the Introduction.

     My reflections and comments, will be indented and italicized and often within the storyline and in a block of text. The comments may not be chronological.

- The stronger demonic activities, those sequences, will be bulleted like the bullet to the upper left and in this size font and justified.

Commanding the spirits, will be in Bold.

     Each chapter will be followed by a ***"Looking back, an Overview"*** and ***"Thoughts to take Away"*** sections. These are meant to help explain, explore and refine this book. They are intended to aid the reader to remain in the overall flow of the story, and offer insights and comments that otherwise might be missed or just not written into the storyline itself.

Chapter-Eight

- The Demons Assault -

I was sitting in my living room and wondering why I felt the need to call Walter; it was such an intense feeling that day. I didn't call him too often as our conversations quickly went off into his delusions and fantasies. Nothing ever changed with Walter; it was always unsettling to speak with him. I wrote letters now and then, and sent money monthly to try to give him something of a break. All told; there was little family left for me as most of my relations had passed on. Remember the folks across the tracks from the Adams family (In book one, page 4). That has some utility here, here in my story. The best part of my relations with the few family members I still had, was the frequent prayers sent up for them and my occasional visits. About a week from when I'd noticed that odd, strongly compelling urge to call Walter. I got a condolence note from an adult home where Walter stayed. This was at Rockaway Beach in Queens, New York. So I tried calling to locate him, and eventually tracked him down to a hospital's on-site adult home. And was told he had died about ten days earlier.

Boy that was tough; conversations with Walter always left me in a somewhat agitated condition, knowing I couldn't do anything to help him. He had lived in such a sad state of delusion. However, I did manage to get Walter buried in the family plot, intercepting his remains before they were interred in NYC's Hart Island, along with a million other unattended graves. More about Walter later. Shortly after that strange things started happening. I prayed a lot and often in tongues then and I began getting "self-interpretations" that were tremendously encouraging and beautiful. It was as though the Holy Spirit had decided that it was my time, a time for me to get truly well plugged in. Sometimes though, what I'd hear when interpreting tongues was just too beautiful and that made me wonder. As for this praying in tongues and allowing who I initially thought was the real Holy Spirit, to use my tongue to provide an interpretation. I continued to suspect this phenomenon and wondered who the source was.

While wanting to check this out, I decided to use a holiday due me at work, an architectural consultancy, and see what I could find. I got my Sportster loaded up and well packed adding a healthy selection of pain pills for sore buns, and planned out a trip to Austin Texas, to see Rob and his wife Lisa. Traveling long distance on a Harley Sportster was a challenge and one that I thoroughly enjoyed. With a 3 ½ gallon peanut tank. About one and a half hours between gas stops and I was moving right along. Twelve hour days of riding, passing trucks, listening to the exhaust tone and the feel of the road, and Hosanna the boots fit the foot pegs awfully well. Good boots and there was no effort in keeping my feet on the pegs, I just kept running along. "Sporties" can be such good clean fun - thoroughly enjoyable! Mine had a sweet spot around 72 mph; it ran so smoothly there. Occasionally while motoring along and thinking, or analyzing recent events, I'd stop alongside the road for prayer and to chill out for a bit. For me, that day, this trip was undertaken to set a series of fleeces, testing what I'd heard. I'd heard such wondrous things that it was time to check them out. If I'd heard right maybe there was a change of vocation coming and I wanted to know if my interpretations truly were of God. You see the supposed "holy spirit" was saying "I needed to get closer to him," for me to walk out all that he had for me. These were wonderful things, but not always. Once, a rather strange thing happened. And the spirit behind the interpretation said that I needed to get closer to him so I could be "strong enough," as coming events would involve some sort of conflict "in the Church?" Other times, I heard different "hard things" that were difficult to understand and digest. I needed to learn more about this powerful spirit.

There was a principle being worked with here, and I was to understand it over time, it was pretty simple and devilishly complicated all at once. That law is this. When a "spirit of deception" is at work against a person, trying to interrogate it with biblical texts to see what the spirit is – (i.e., testing the spirits,) just won't work. It's extremely difficult to determine what's what. But, at some point the demons will expose themselves. Here's the reason for this: it's an experiment on their part, a challenge and a test of our willingness to oppose them. Should the demons reveal themselves, and you don't respond by aggressively coming against them in the opposite spirit, combating them with all you know to do. You're passively accepting their presence, and you just upped their permissions to come against you! And by effectively empowering them you're coming closer to agreement with them. And that's an extremely precarious position for you to be in. They want to be in authority, over you! The true God, Holy Spirit (the real Holy Spirit) sets limits on the oppression, he won't let them overwhelm you, experience taught me that. But, you can affect those limits by your choices; you can be all on your own, you can isolate yourself from the Holy Spirit. That is if you yield your will to your enemy. The demons will bait and entrap you at every opportunity you let them; you can bank on it; understand the suckers and fight!

- So it was down to Austin Texas, on the Sporty. Eventually, I pulled into town; it was around 4:00 PM and traffic was getting thick. Everything was routine, and all at once the handlebars were jerked free of my hands and the bike took off. I was shooting off the freeway at 50-mph. Mouth open, eyes wide, startled and alarmed. I was charging down the raised and grass covered highway embankment onto a dirt trail found there. Then I was sprinting down that footpath and across two full lanes of one way traffic, stopped at a stop sign, facing me. I caught a glimpse of the car drivers they looked as alarmed as me. Then another lane, the outer one in my direction it was clear. I jammed across that and flew into a gas station and slid skidding heart pounding up to a pump; what the...? If I wasn't a well-seasoned and really skilled rider I'd be dead, what the heck was that...?

I've heard preachers and different leaders dismiss the "enemy" as someone you don't have to be concerned with. Well, it's hard not to think of some choice words; words unfit to print here whenever I hear that nonsense. I'm going to wander off the storyline, just for a bit. As I'd like to highlight how dangerous demons can be! Especially after writing about my motorcycling incident.

Months after my first stent was implanted, and I was still working with Freddy, I had recovered enough that the ache in my arms was all but gone, and I was walking well. I decided I needed more exercise and started working out on an old Nordic Track at the apartment. I had been told by my cardio guy to do whatever I wanted, yes Paul, go climb Horsetooth Mountain, ride bicycles, run, whatever! Today, now, I don't listen to those cardio guys so much - Enough already! It's asking the Lord, use my common sense and search internet medical sites. I'm doing much better now.

- To continue, one night I couldn't get to sleep, nothing doing; I kept getting stitches in my side, gas, backaches, intense muscle aches and headaches. There was no way to get a bit of sleep. Morning came; and I was exhausted. Then, sitting on the edge of the bed thinking "How am I going to work like this?" An idea hits me. "I know, I'll work my way through this on the Nordic Track!" I groggily stumbled into the other room, got the treadmill in motion, and was about a minute on the thing when my heart stopped. Uh-oh. Then, in a moment it began beating again, "oh, good." Then, it stopped again, and I thought "this is not good." And it started going again. I slowly, terribly weakly, just barely wobbled my way to a chair and sat there. Concentrating on breathing, waiting, hoping to feel better. It took me a full year to recover, at first it was exhausting just climbing the six steps to my apartment. I've no idea how much I spent on nutritional supplements but I did manage to slog my way back and return to work. Yeah, "Pay no attention to the man behind the screen!" Said the man behind the screen remembering that classic old movie "The Wizard of Oz."

That was a full-on demonic ambush, and it worked very well, for them. The enemy tried to kill me on various occasions. Boy do I despise those things, and of course I had no idea at that time of what was happening. Yeah, "pay no attention," said the man behind the screen. As far as the motorcycle was concerned, I'd been riding on and off since I was nineteen, early on as an "Outlaw" biker. I didn't drive a car until I was twenty seven; I've since crisscrossed all across the US. I've even ridden some in West Africa and Europe and survived with Colorado plates in Normandy, France. And at no other time have handlebars been jerked out of my grasp no matter how rough the road, not once; it's the man behind the screen! So the trip to Austin continued, and I was heavily under deception, and without enough clues to understand this, not yet. I'd enjoyed my visit with the Joys and had a good time in Austin. Old friends are invaluable and could have been consulted, but this was personal.

And the time for confronting this had not arrived yet. "This, proof of the pudding," was still in the "what's this tasting like?" stage. On my way back to Colorado I stopped to pray and then pray some more, and then in tongues and tried interpreting. And then got some encouraging info, a check should be waiting, cool it was needed. Another twelve hour day of riding and I as I approached Fort Collins I had to grin, I'd made good time and it was still daylight, ah yes, sighing, home again. Then I checked the mail and found nothing? I remember thinking. Huh, oh OK I'll wait until tomorrow. I was tired then and it was time to put things away, change the oil on the scoot and clean the thing up, chores to do. The next day arrived chores got finished; the postman came and no delivery. Huh, once again? Later in the day I was praying and thinking on the fleeces and wandering about the house. And decided this was interpretations business was all deception and the author had to be of the enemy. And boo on that tongue. I prayed again, interpreted and told the spirit behind the interpretations that I wanted nothing more to do with it and that it is a liar and cannot be of God.

- Then a voice came from out of nowhere, and as loud as could be, shouting, *"WHAT? YOU DARE TO CALL US LIARS!"* The volume, the intensity, the low pitch of that voice were such that I was pummeled and shaking. Physically made to grab onto something and just hang on. I'd been powerfully blasted by this voice, like a doubled barreled shotguns recoil when it's held too loosely. Or like a bullhorn, blowing straight into the ear. Then, I was hit with such anxiety that my stomach started turning. I experienced nausea and depression, and my back muscles rolled up with tension everything got confused, and the world started spinning a bit, and this happened all-together and all at once! And this thing was screaming at me. Loud as a cranked up stereo! *"YOU DARE TO CONFRONT US!!"* Tears were streaming down my face from the intense back pain; the muscles were all twisted into knots! I'd not experienced anything remotely like this before. Wow, I was in trouble and what the heck could I do?

- This thing was continually yelling at me. **"So, you're a Christian; so what? You're going to do what you're told, or it's going to get lots worse!** *HOW DARE YOU CONFRONT US?"* So it began. The demon told me what to do, and I did the opposite. I tried casting it

65

out, and it laughed at me and taunted me. **"I'm in - I'm out - I'm in your mind. Nope, alongside you." "You cannot escape; you're going to be dragged straight to Hell!"** *"CHRISTIAN MAN!"*

This was my new day, full-on spiritual warfare, and there was no escaping it. They just keep talking, lecturing, badgering, plotting and annoying me, there was always something it was a constant. And then, then there were new ones showing up, groan. The current debate right then was between different railing spirits working together, trying to compel me to obedience. Oh great, and now these new ones were taking turns, and this would not stop.

Here's an illustration that I offered a person after she looked me right in the eye, and said, "Just tell them to shut up Paul." Try to imagine this. You are standing next to a freeway on-ramp where the ramp curves up to meet the freeway. Its late night and the cars have their lights on. You're standing by the curve where the headlamps hit you full on, and your eyes hurt from the glare. You, you put your hands up commanding. "In the name of the Lord Jesus Christ glaring car headlights, stop!" Yeah right, lots of luck to you sir! But people still didn't get it. There was nothing I could do! After some days, things leveled off a bit. The high volume yelling finally ceased, and the voices were more at a conversational level, voices that were always present, talking, plotting, accusing, and taunting.

I called my Pastor and got an appointment ten days away, nothing urgent here, sigh, got to have an appointment. Over the next ten days I was on the Internet all the time, trying to find anything that would help me. But it was mostly useless; I'm a Christian man, and I can't get demons; I just cannot have any demons; nice to know that! My poor brother Walter, now I understand what his doctors were trying to block out with drugs. I tried whatever I could find back then trying to sleep. I was getting, maybe, two hours a night. And was so exhausted and so severely haunted that I knew for a certainty that no one was likely to understand. And the demons were still yakking away, lecture after lecture, and then another stinking lecture, and "you're going to get free, ha! There's no hope for you, Christian man, with your sins!"

An inspector type spirit came by, "what's going on here how come he's not in Hell?" He's threatened to take charge and crank up the persecution, this should have been over weeks ago; the wicked spirit said. I could imagine the inspector; deep voiced a cigar smoker, frumpy, wearing a cheap suit with a stack of folders on his desk, boo. The strangest thing was this: I'm Paul D. Moehring, quite sane. This wasn't me talking, and I know that the Lord God is real, and this is all going to be used, somehow, for my good, right?? That's what the Bible says so it's got to be true. I've been there; I've worked it through, and I know that God's word is true! The problem is; I also know that people cannot go without sleep, and I can't find anything that will help me sleep. At last, I got to see my pastor, he heard what I had to say. He related that he had a demon once, and it just went away. And he looked a little afraid it might come back. So then, he quoted some scripture and looked at me like something was supposed to have happened. Then he laid hands on me, prayed and looked at me like something was supposed to have happened, again. Then, he tried talking in tongues for a bit, and I got a little relief - better than nothing, and that was it! It lasted about twenty minutes, lots of luck I sighed.

I jumped on my Sporty and went for a ride through the Colorado Rocky Mountains swooping through some corners; it's certainly entertaining living twenty minutes from the twisties. The things were still yapping away, but so what, boo on them; I can still enjoy motorcycling despite them all. It's a sanity machine! My best friends in Austin suggested I see some friends of theirs who had a deliverance ministry back then. I knew them a bit, and well - maybe they could help. I showed up a few days later, and they had me fill out a several page questionnaire. Then, they went after a few spirits that they thought might have been about; they knew the names of them, but no joy from that. The demons within me were laughing at them and taunting me, saying they were not even a threat to them. Then this gentleman that meant no harm and knew no better, started wandering about. He was flapping his arms and began happily relating how he was getting invigorated from all this Holy Ghost tongue talking; he was babbling away and as far as I could tell this was accomplishing nothing. Was this deliverance? His wife did her thing next.

And offered some bum advice, I had spoken about seeing a Jesus looking figure seeming to be involved. There was nothing holy about seeing that figure though, projected at me by the demons. Anything goes with the things; they'll try any trick imaginable. One of the ways they try to disturb the objects of their warfare is to project mental images. These are images you will eventually realize are false; it's a trap. Evil spirits will go to extraordinary lengths to discourage and embarrass a believer, and having looked to a false image can accomplish some great discouragement, some real confusion, you bet. I wasted a few weeks with these folks. They did try, but they were not what they wished to be and of no help. They quickly lost interest in trying to help me, and I lost any hope of getting any effective help from them. But they did do one thing for me; I asked the gentleman if he knew of anyone who had an "effective" deliverance ministry. And he suggested I contact Bro. Mel, who had a Barbecue place in town.

Next day, I got in the car and went to Bro Mel's "Southern Style - Barbecue Restaurant" - "Put Some South in your Mouth" prominently displayed and introduced myself. Bro Mel came over to my table and we talked for quite a while. I told him the story of this sorry affair and my needing real help, as this was such a strongly focused and unrelenting attack, and not getting any better! Basically, I ended our conversation by saying "I'm just a Christian man who has tried to serve the Lord and was doing my best. Were this horror to go away I'd probably go back to missions, as that is one place I'd enjoyed and had been a bit useful in." Bro Mel gave me his card and directions to his church and said to come by that Sunday. I suppose he must have been looking at one weird and whacked-out guy. I barely had any control over my emotions. I was continually being assaulted by demons, gleefully engaged in working me over. Man, this so very much sucketh! If I were to walk into any public health official's office and tell him of my day, I would be forcibly confined for my safety. I needed to avoid those guys this was demons, and I just wanted to shout; I'm fine.

I'm still me no matter what these things do.

"Looking Back, an Overview"

≈≈≈

The nature of this warfare is mental. It's your mind and emotions opposing the minds of the demon powers. They demand to be in control, daily demonstrating their ability to inflict suffering. It's their lone lever. All else is illusion and lies. It's warfare exercised by stealth or conflict and it's always about. It's ongoing and incessant. It's always in operation at some level, somewhere, somehow, its life in this long fallen world.

"Thoughts to Take Away"

≈≈≈

It's essential in this warfare, to get real. Discard all illusions. I'd bet there's no one at the door, standing there with a ready solution in hand prepared to help. You've got to Get-Busy.

Chapter-Nine

- All Nations Church -

OK, Sunday arrived, and I was off to All Nations Church and Deliverance Center, 1412 Webster, Fort Collins, Colorado. This location is in a working class neighborhood close by the local municipal airport. Nearby were car repair and auto parts franchises, some small stores and a good motorcycle shop. Then restaurants and just lots of every day type places. The church itself is an ordinary storefront in a typical small strip. Outside, it was nothing special, it was all on the inside where the special is. Deliverance is a very difficult ministry, and I'm glad I'm not called to be a deliverance minister, But Bro Mel was. And this is so unusual an effective ministry in a challenging arena. When the church's services had concluded, Bro Mel asked if I wanted prayer and pointed to a chair at the foot of the podium. I walked up, sat down, and wondered what this was all about. He explained that what he did was called "Confrontational Deliverance," and he was going to get in my face. He was going to call out the demons. Commanding them to identify themselves by name.

My job was to report accurately what I heard. I still think Bro Mel wasn't quite prepared for my reporting, as I heard the things so very clearly. Sometimes, he misinterpreted like when the things were yelling that they were going to kill me, I reported it, and he thought they meant him. This Confrontational Deliverance was a Holy Spirit empowered method of calling out the spirits. Commanding them to speak out their names, taking their history - when wanted, and then casting them out. Bro Mel kept nailing those rotten spirits; that is the ones that were getting gathered up and cast out. It had to have been the power of the Holy Spirit. Bro Mel would call them out and have them tell on themselves and at other times, well not so much. Sometimes the higher powered demons would sacrifice the littler ones. They would hide behind them or shove them into the line of fire! Bless Bro Mel, as he delivered me till around 1:00 am, and we were both utterly exhausted.

- Bro Mel went home to sleep, and I went home to be persecuted by demons. "We're going to tear you apart when you walk in the door," they'd say. I'd spend hours quoting scriptures and trying all I could think to do, desperately attempting to fend them off - hoping to get some sleep. Maybe I'd get a few hours, and then I'd be awakened by something unexpected. One morning I awoke sitting bolt upright. I'd been blasted. The filthy things had powerfully imitated the sounds of a Fort Collins diesel-electric train. (There's a switching track running through the center of town.) And the engine's horns were blaring, like at a railroad crossing and the steel wheels were screeching as they do. Then, just to add a delightful topping. The demons combined that train's racket, with the sensation of my being on my Harley Sportster and being powerfully buffeted by wind from trucks in the oncoming lane, like at highway speeds, boom! Wow... all I could do was sit there for a while, just rocking and shaking violently. This was getting deadly. As the Christmas Holidays approached; I prevailed upon Bro Mel to come over to my place and deliver me. I didn't think I would survive the holidays without help. If I couldn't sleep at all, my real mind, the one that was being assaulted, might just crumble or my ticker might give out. I couldn't see any way out. Bro Mel and the church's worship leader George, met me at the house just as I was returning from the store, and I gladly let them in. They liked my house; it was roomy and clean, and I'd gotten fresh coffee for them. We got right to work.

- Bro Mel found plenty of spirits to cast out, and then he found a terrific one - a watching spirit connected to a coven. The filthy thing would stand in the hallway right by my bedroom and inform its coven of the best times to attack. This deliverance brought me such relief that I could get a bit of restful sleep. Without Bro Mel's help on that occasion I might have snapped. When Bro Mel went after that watching spirit, I could have sworn that I saw it go straight up bursting right through the roof. "Wow, what is the depth to this?" I thought. I learned later that a boatload of spirits departing from Walter came straightaway to me at his passing. There were demons expelled during my deliverance that claimed to be the ones that killed him. Demons lie, but they also tell the truth. That is when it serves them. Demons also like to twist things if they can, so who can tell what's what? And in the final analysis of things, who cares. So long as they're getting cast out. But, once again, I come from a demonized family, which means

I've been vulnerable to the things from the moment of conception. What the heck...? Boy, life can be downright unfriendly, and just setup for all kinds of low and mean failures.

The sad fact of the matter is that the demons had built a stronghold like a spiritual fortress. They can establish these strongholds in anyone with vulnerabilities, with doors left open for their entry. They require consenting permissions to enter, which may be as simple a thing as believing a lie, all the way to not repenting of some grievous sin. The demons could shelter under those legal excuses and thrive. And then there was this, the most insidious part of our inherited iniquities. In effect, we're stuck with the consequences of someone else's sins. So a nasty haunting could start from there too. So once again, there was hidden in me somewhere, someplace, a top level spiritual stronghold. One which was comprised of many more strongholds and multiple defenses. "Defenses in depth," defenses populated by scads & scads of demons, whole armies. It seems that within me was a construction project, a project so vast. (That to their diabolical minds.) Overseen by their leaders the prince demons, there was no way I was going to get free. If they couldn't beat me into doing their demonic missions with them, they would kill me. This was their master plan. The genuine reality, the whole truth is this: "That all authority belongs to the Lord Jesus Christ." Jesus of Nazareth obtained that power at such an enormous cost, for us, at Golgotha. And he has given us all that strength and ability and means for us to use it. And I had to learn how to do that and I would! I had committed myself to fight them for as long as I had breath, and that was my full intent. It was an easy position to take. I hadn't learned about iniquities, not yet. But I knew that a self-defense for me was going to mean sanctification and purging, as the Word says we're to do. And I also knew this. That I was the last of my family line on both sides, and sometimes, sometimes I wondered when some blessings might kick in as I sure was aware of the curses.

So Wednesdays and Sundays were deliverance time at church, and they were a source of help. Many other days, the Sporty and I would be seen out and about in the Fort. Or up high in the mountains as that was one place where the things were of little influence, and I truly enjoyed that scoot. I was also in a good position as I had the time, experience, and the desire to research through the XLForum.com.

73

A Spiritual Warfare Ensemble

A website that was a chat room populated by a group of Sportster riders worldwide, and with a user generated and searchable database. I happily engaged in researching performance issues, learning how to improve on the factory's meager suspension efforts, so-so tires and such. The rest of my time was frequently spent on spiritual warfare. The recession had hit CPP Wind, the wind tunnel and architectural consultancy where I worked, and I was laid off along with a third of the staff. I deserved it as the demons had made things difficult for me at work too. It may seem odd, but many severely demonized folks can do well at work, and that's because they're so involved in earning their livelihood that it's hard for the demons to break through. But that's not always the case; there was this one incident that happened shortly before my layoff.

- One day at work, the demons decided to show me their power, so as I went about the building performing the network maintenance and user support roles. Everywhere I went, the directors and senior engineers were bowing, smiling, and congratulating me. It was weird. Many of the principals resented having a LAN administrator with my high wages. They didn't understand what it took to keep the systems running well and undervalued my work. My boss understood and genuinely liked what I was doing. And here were all these high powered folks, some world leaders in their fields. Others were even active Christian's, worship leaders and suchlike, shaking hands and complimenting me! Wow, those darn spirits, they certainly could shape things! They could even make it seem as though they could be of some use in doing valuable and decent things for you. Boy, I cannot imagine how steep a price would be required for a service like that!

The upside of my unwanted unemployment was that I routinely collected unemployment benefits electronically while I tried my best to find work. Then I'd ride the bike for a break and engage the demons in spiritual warfare, sometimes ten hours a day, or night, the things were getting a hard aggressive fight from me. I had the time then, and I was still myself still sane, loving the Lord and trusting in Him. I was spending many hours a week on the Internet, and I was always reading and looking for methods and any practical way to work out my sanctification.

And all this time, I had this ongoing dialog aimed at me from the demons with their traps inherent. They were well skilled at setting me up for conflicts with them, and there was this constant roller coaster, one of where my emotions were manipulated without my consent or control. What was downright awful, was half the time I didn't have a chance to prepare myself, like when I came back to the house after church, I knew they'd be waiting. But other times what came at me was a total surprise; it was as fluid as words and thoughts could be. The attacks could be quite subtle, planned out over time and most always, they were unexpected.

- Then, there was this continual struggle for sleep. One night I was just about asleep, and I remember a spirit saying, "Hey Paul, I've got something for you." Huh, what? "I don't want anything from you!" And then I heard, "we're going to show you our world." Someone was chuckling, and I felt myself getting lighter and lighter, and gradually coming up, lifting up and off my bed, and in my horror I started calling out to Jesus, Jesus, Jesus. There is such power in that name, and I fell back on the bed and the attack was broken. That scared the socks off me! That was a trip I would not want to make. Then there was the additional threat of an early morning wake-up call. One morning I awoke, feeling the mattress shaking and getting booted, boom! I was kicked right out of bed, standing there and looking about, what the…? Many nights, I experienced something like this: Late at night, I would try to concentrate on just relaxing, shucking off the events of the day. I would have some anticipation of drifting off to sleep, sometimes it worked.

- Then, I would get a mental picture; one that wouldn't go away; it just kept building. Gradually out of the corners of my mind, I would see a small group of spirit-looking guys, with white hospital style smocks and tools, chainsaws and levers, crowbars and such. They would approach me and stop at my head. Then, they would go to work hacking at my head and my brain and say they're going to take me apart! I couldn't get this image out of my mind; it was like being stuck, resentfully watching a video. This scene would last for quite a while, and it was downright awkward feeling this nonsense going on. Eventually, a voice would say, "Well, that's about it for tonight, the Holy Spirit says we have to stop!" So, they would pack up their tools and slowly wander out of sight. Then this harassing voice would continue on, lecture after lecture, gradually diminishing. "So, you're going to get free, Christian man?" "How are you going to do that with your brain in pieces, tell me that Christian guy?"

• On another night, right about when I first started attending All Nations Church I was dead beat, just exhausted and about to get to sleep. When a spirit said loudly, "I want you to meet the boss." Gradually a strong tension built. Huh? I'm felt like I was about to fall off a cliff. What the heck…? Then I saw a robed and hooded figure coming, black robed, nasty and menacing, and my emotions were going off the wall. I was terrified. But of what. Huh? The demons were slamming my emotions. The spirit said "meet the boss. His name is Satan." Then this hooded image leered at me, and I got alarmed and angry and got in its face. "I belong to the Lord Jesus Christ; I've been bought at a price, and you can go get stuffed!" This thing reared back and solemnly pronounced, "This Christian man has rebuffed the lord of this world and is approved as a man of God." And on and on. Gradually, the harassment slowed, and I got to sleep. The following night it was much the same deal. "Rats," like Lucy, of the Peanuts comic strip would say. But this time, about the end of my power encounter with "Satan." I recognized what was being played out. In this staged-play, this assault, the "Satan" I was encountering was an image from the Disney movie, Snow White and the Seven Dwarfs. It was the evil witch character! Aha got ya. That's not the real deal, stupid spirits! But boy, those demons, they skillfully staged this whole thing, and they sure messed with me - I was terrified. And it's no sleep again. It was a mixed bag of attacks, and I had no idea of the enemy's numbers. I just knew that Walter spent one-third of his life in mental institutions, and they had to be real sinks of demonic activity; I'd gotten a bunch.

I read a book from a pastor that's spent forty plus years fighting for people against wicked spirits, and he stated that schizophrenia is entirely demonic. In discussing this with people that know the demonic, they proposed. "That the demons can do such physical damage to the brain. That the damages from their attacks, are the physical symptoms that science notes and flags and medical doctors attempt to treat." They have no concept of the roots of this horror, natural or supernatural.

I remember reading a story in the New York Times, about an experimental schizophrenia drug made by recombinant techniques. Scientists were synthesizing enzymes in the brain that could prompt schizophrenic episodes, or stop them. The drug worked well in its tests, and they reported how terribly oppressed, straitjacketed patients would be given the drug and shortly after obtain a healthy mental state. The schizophrenics would report being so relieved, and so overjoyed at their new freedom from the voices and anxiety and depression. Then, the trial ended, and they gradually and painfully went back to their straitjackets, desperately pleading for help along the way. The problem with the drug was the extreme cost; it was $1,500 per treatment at that time. This being haunted by demon powers; this condition is no joke; it's a terrible situation for anyone to be caught in. All I could do was to stay with my faith in the Lord Jesus Christ and fight, day after day, every day. Things varied, and the blasted demons were skilled, mentally alert and had a bag full of tricks. Regarding demonic attacks on the church, the Apostle Paul once said; "they knew his tricks." But in my time, well not so much. I continued to sit in the chair at All Nations Church and fought back with Bro Mel. I went for deliverance on Wednesdays and Sundays and then back to the house for that night's abuse. Altogether I must have sat in that chair at every opportunity I could get for over a year. After that, there was someone new, someone I supposed I should defer to in Christian charity, many weeks on. And from then on, I started to rely on self-deliverance more and more.

At the house, I worked at not reacting to their plots. I dedicated myself to coming against them in the opposite spirit, a term I first heard from Deyon Stephens, who co-founded Mercy Ships. She offered no explanation at the time, but it resonated with me, and I adopted it. For instance, I used it this time when the demons attempted to take my Sporty away. I was told that enough was enough and that I'd used that bike as an escape from their harassment too many times. "Be afraid!" they'd say. And I was told they would keep me from riding "by any means!" Next day, I decided that a ride was in order and got the bike out of the garage. But I could hardly get it down the driveway and to the street, my head was spinning so. I was hit with such a powerful attack of confusion that I lost all sense of balance, and was walking like a drunk. I couldn't even walk a straight line or see clearly.

So what, "I'll look through one eye I thought" I'll not let them control me; there's no way. So I got the bike started and pointed in the right direction and underway. Lots of years riding in advanced states of intoxication as a biker came to my aid, and I was off, heading to the nearby Rocky Mountains, the twisties. I headed out of town and went around the local watersports recreational areas, Horsetooth Mountain, and its lake. Then, through the local mountain villages, it was all good road with lots of tight turnings and very little traffic. I picked up Route I-34 to Estes Park, which starts at the edge of Loveland Township and traverses mountain passes. Winding through the occasional hamlet, and deeply wooded mountainous sections with all manner of twists and turns and sweepers, some even banked. It's cheating to use the bikes brakes on roads like this; the gearbox is the way to go, using the engine as a brake when needed. Mostly engine-braking when rapidly coming into a turn. Enjoying hearing the deceleration in the exhaust pipes, then to the apogee of the turn and roll the throttle on, pushing and pulling on the handlebars and wind that engine up, swiftly power shifting! Then, touch the front brake lever, lightly, drop the bike down in the front fork tubes and setup for the next turn. Up and down through the gears and there was always a grin on my face, and pee on the demons. I'd enjoyed this too much; they'd lost, again. Fight them in any way you can; always do battle with them. Do it by defying and outwitting them; that's the best of an opposite spirit. Stand up to them at all times, confound them!

- Another time I countered them with the opposite spirit: was one night when the filthy things were really after me. They'd gotten my back muscles in bunches, again. And I was getting pounded by oppression and depression and nausea and headed to the computer. I'd found a website with a listing of demonic spirits, and I could go after them by their functions and attempt to cast the relevant ones out. I was sitting there in front of the display, panting and exhausted, messed up by all the attacks and just from walking down the hall to the computer. My head was spinning and down from the beating, I was so darned tired! Then I remembered that in their lecturing that day, they'd told me they were going to break me, and then it would really get rough. Oh yeah, enough! I popped my head up and got after the top ones on the list. Then I heard the demons gasp, and the attack broke, just like a dry stick. They didn't think I had it in me. They took their best shot and thought they'd broken me, but I sent them packing. Thank you Lord, I didn't know I had it in me either, bless you, bless you.

I'm telling you the history of my oppression so that you can appreciate what the Lord has done for me. Some might think I make too much of this, and that I should sit in the back in church and keep the bench warm. Well, no I will not. Put this book down if you think learning about your enemy's tactics and abilities is something to be lightly dismissed. As, well, you'd not like to "give glory" to the enemy. Glorify them? Not very likely! Call them out; sort them out and cast the lot out! Understand and fight.

But I've heard that demonic oppression is such a "Rare" thing?

Really!... let's see. The prisons are full of people coming from the ranks of abused children, plenty of drug abuses, sexual abuse's etc., up there at the big house. Yup, plenty of room for demonic activity there. Mental institutions house a bunch of people hearing voices and folks with out-of-control emotions. I'd say I know something of that, and yes - there's room for the demonic there, most certainly. The local phone book has a whole bunch of psychiatrists and therapists and sometimes Christian counselors listed in every town of any size. So I'd say there's more than a fair chance for some demonic activity there too. I remember a late 2012, New York Times article in Google News. Lamenting the poor state of mental health in the US, and stating the following. "That you would never guess what the fifth and sixth best-selling prescription drugs are in the United States, so I'll just tell you: They are Abilify and Seroquel, two powerful antipsychotics. In 2011 alone, they and other antipsychotic drugs were prescribed to 3.1 million Americans at a cost of $18.2 billion, a 13 percent increase over the previous year." Additionally, in a quote from a 2013, Wall Street Journal article, "20 percent of Americans now take a psychiatric drug on a daily basis.

We have 11 percent of our youth diagnosed with ADHD; we have this great expansion in bipolar diagnosis, and from a societal point of view. Rather than the burden on mental illness decreasing in these past 30 years, it's greatly expanded in terms of the numbers of people in treatment and their disabilities." But really folks, c'mon now. With a divorce rate at about the same rate as the world. With church splits, broken marriages, ministries taken to pieces from feuding, sexual degeneracy, money problems and untimely deaths among God's people. It looks like; there is more than a "mere possibility," that wicked spirits are at work! Over the years, I've talked with the children of pastors and noticed that their difficulties can be just as intense as any other group of people. So, where's God's protection? Doesn't it work broadly? For households, for layman's kids, pastors kids? Could it be that God's protection depends on us using it! Let's explore this subject just for a bit. Even if only a small group of people (let's say the convinced, committed Chris-

tians). Would recognize that mental, physical, emotional, rela-
tional, financial, and other long-running family problems. (Remember the family tree opposite the Adams family tree back in
Chapter One.) Can have their roots, deep, rotten roots. And
those roots can later blossom into many problems and diseases
that are not brought on by their lack of exercise, dietary defi-
ciencies, etc., and are certainly not of the Holy Spirit. And that
there isn't even the slightest chance of those roots being implanted by circumstances and oddities, their just flukes, that's
a nope. Then, recognize that here must be sufficient room for demonic oppression! Really. And at that point, realize that those
deep dark, rotten roots, actually exist. And investigate, identify,
and destroy them! Then the church might begin a shifting from
just an audience to more of an army.

So maybe the part that's ACTUALLY "rare," is when
God's people recognize their need for help. And then find it! And
I mean help that's hard hitting, effective and well organized.
And, yes, I will show you how. But first, let's get some idea of
the real depth of this. And please keep in mind folks, I'm not
stupid; I've just been picked on, quite a lot my brothers and sis-
ters; that's all.

"Looking back, an Overview"

≈≈

During all of my troubles, I kept wondering: If it's true that I can't be alone in this, where's everyone else? Where's the practicality of God's defenses for us and how do I implement them? How do I proceed, who can I talk to and what can I read?

– Please pass this book on –

"Thoughts to take Away"

≈≈

This rather odd book, this examination of my troubles, proves that if nothing else, that spiritual warfare is real. This book is what it is, and I'm who I present myself to be, warts and all. Everything is just as it happened. My life in this far fallen world.

Chapter-Ten

- The Resistance -

The war continued; Pastor Mel had his barbecue restaurant, and I started stopping by there when the place got quiet and we'd talk. I liked it that on leaving there, the wicked spirits were in such an agitated state of consternation; I would just grin. I was fighting them about every chance I could get; that is, apart from my daily warfare which I'd put on a schedule. Bro Mel asked insightful questions and was a potent source for counseling. Even though, sometimes, he must have misunderstand what I was trying to convey. How was I supposed to talk about all this stuff? It was pretty hard trying to figure all this out! And how to do that without confusing someone else? – I was often confused – though seldom clueless, I think now. It took a while for Bro. Mel to appreciate what the actual level of my infestation was, and he's been doing deliverance for nearly twenty-five years! This man was overworked, with his restaurant and the ministry that sometimes lasted half the night. God Bless his heart! Sometimes, it seemed like, that despite all of our efforts, I'm was making too little progress.

- It was late and time for sleep, I'd stayed up late on the computer thinking maybe I could nod off, that is if tired enough. Eventually I tried going to bed. It was a nice queen sized bed with a too firm mattress to which I'd added a very soft, 3" Latex topper, and it was actually quite sweet. A voice popped up then and said. "Hey, Paul; I've got a present for you," I quickly and emphatically replied, "No, no, absolutely not, I don't want any gifts from you. You keep your presents." The light from the street lamp just down the road was coming in the bedroom window and I could see pretty clearly. And then my present arrived. And I could see the impressing's of an invisible form, slowly lying down. Starting at the foot of the bed, partially on the bed and partly - ON ME. It impressed the very soft latex topper, and I could see it quite clearly shifting about and revealing itself in the latex by its curves, its shape overall. And it was crawling up - ON ME. I plainly understood its form by the deepening impression it left, the feel of it and just a bit of weight, and it was evil, cloying, female and so nasty! I sprang up, shaking with revulsion.

- I quickly got into motion, heading to the computer to try to find help, lots of luck I thought then. It was riding on my back, and the spirit that prompted this was laughing and having a grand time. And I thought as I trudged to the computer, "how will I search for this online?" Nothing came to mind and what the heck, so I stopped and prayed, "Dear Lord, please send this thing back to where it came from," nothing. Then I commanded it, "In **the name of the Lord Jesus Christ, go back to the spirit that sent you to me!**" Score, and it was gone, fabulous. Ah good, that's so neat, and that ratfink spirit that demonic dunce that instigated this attack on me. It was screaming loudly. He was running around and away, and it was stuck fast, clinging to him, good! I discussed this the next day with Bro Mel, and he said, "Stop that. You're using the same witchcraft that sent it to you." "So, what do I do now?" Rats. Fortunately, the thing did not return, but the spirit that sent it to me surfaced, complaining it was on him all night! Good, cool, suffer!

Those demons, they must have been extremely busy orchestrating their plans, and again, there was a coup coming, sigh. With my usual, (low and seemingly nil) spiritual batting average, I swung and missed, I just didn't see it coming. Most nights it's some variation on ignoring the attacks against me or quoting scripture after scripture without effect as I just get worn out, and they always kept coming. I was still stuck (reluctantly) listening to the constant and unwelcome lectures, plots, traps, and general commentary that hit me. Most nights, it wasn't until the Holy Spirit said "enough is enough." Gradually, the things would quiet down some and I would get to sleep. I couldn't stop the imagination; they managed that in me when they attacked, I saw what they wanted me to. Typically, they'd see the same things as I did. I know that's quite a statement, but you see I've discerned how to get information from them; it's mostly from learning when to pay attention. I usually tried to avoid paying any attention to them, not at all. Since whatever it was they wanted to express, it was, well, way beyond quite-suspect. Sometimes, though. They explained themselves truthfully, often doing so in trying to make a point.

For instance, confusion. Confusion is something they're quite adept at introducing. Like when it's difficult to figure out if your thoughts are your own or theirs. You think, "Am I thinking clearly right now, or are they are interfering here as well." It's hard to know what's what in bad times like these, what's inter- ference and what's truly me? But, know this, no matter how deeply they oppress a person they cannot eliminate them, they cannot replace them. Each person, each soul, is their unique self, and demons can't steal a person; they can't steal you. You're your own master; you are the originator of your own thoughts; you are in command of yourself. And they cannot eliminate that. But, what they can do is hear the thoughts you've thought, and the words you've spoken aloud and they can see what you're seeing. It's as though they are looking at some video being run, one they have no controls for. They cannot affect your original ideas; they cannot read your mind and extract any information. But they can, append, amend, and adjust things by presenting their ideas. And they know you very, very well. How they often work is to introduce ideas and stage emotional and mental plays you have a role in, very subtly, and very quietly. You're stuck seeing and experiencing them, when they spring their "staged plays" on you. Unwillingly or not, and this just simply, majorly, sucks, it's no wonder it's called insanity. They like to do this when you're part way between active consciousness and obtain- ing sleep, and I am learning all of this piecemeal. Despite many hours of researching, I can't find anything on the web or at local bookstores to have a real solution in hand, and I'm still stuck. Nobody's talking about the reality of this, at least no one I can find at this juncture. There are only so many authors you can study at any one time, and I read them over and over for content. Scripture also affirms this, that I will not be hurt by anything more than I can stand, right?? Scripture also states that what I am enduring is common to all men. So I am not overwhelmingly oppressed, and I can't be the only one, right??

At any rate, what was happening is the things (supposedly) were getting sloppy and letting me see them, unbeknownst to them. As unlikely as this was, it seemed to me there was some precedent. When I first started deliverance with Bro Mel, he'd come to a "gate- keeper spirit," and it would tease him by running around and hiding, feeding him other little spirits to cast out. Bro Mel would chase after the thing and just not be able to cast it out; it would slip away. Bro Mel explained that it was like peeling an onion; you just needed to keep peeling the layers off.

And that this spirit was being protected, as it was a power spirit. To explain further, demons live in a hierarchal system. In a person, or the demon's house, the top of the lineup is the prince demon and like in the Mafia, the lower ranked spirits could be sacrificed to protect the top ones. Anyway, this "gatekeeper - deliverance contest" continued for some weeks. I'd get home, and the things would be threatening me, again, and I'd pay no attention and do what I'd planned to do despite all the threats. So late this one night, I was fed up with the day's harassment and decided to get after that gatekeeper spirit. "**In the name of the Lord Jesus Christ, gatekeeper spirit, what is your name?** Come forward, what is your name spirit?" as I went through the self-deliverance process, and I bagged it! I got it; I cast the nasty thing out! So, thank you Lord God, I'd prayed. Thinking that's good as that thing was extra cruel, and as I got that one, I'll go get me some more, and I did too. I threw a number of the things out that night. Several weeks later I was praying and decided to see what I might get a hold of and went to war.

A spirit showed up and said. "Hey Paul, you remember that gatekeeper spirit you got? Well we all got together and decided to stand aside and let you have him as he was such a bully." It was kind of like a; "don't get too proud of yourself old boy" kind of thing. OK, with that gatekeeper incident in mind, I was ticked. The things had given me a very hard time that day. So, while pondering this daily mess I was stuck with, I started thinking about how the demons' feud with each other, and shove lesser spirits forward to be cast out. How they try to trick one another and snitch on each other. It became quite clear that theirs was not a static environment. Their structures were chaotic, dirty, messy, and always entirely spiritual. The demons were malign, intelligent, and very evil wisps of ectoplasm. To us in the natural world, kind of like smoke in a bottle. How many soot particles are there in light smoke? How many more when it's dark and dense? So as it's purely a spiritual environment, to them. The demons must be "mentally aware," and I was thinking that… There's got to be a way to pay them back for the times they so cruelly messed with me! And so I reasoned, that as they use me for a house and are into my mind, I should be able to get into theirs too, right? To expound a bit.

I was crazy; I heard voices, and my emotions were constantly doing something odd. But that's not me; I was fine, so it must be them! Totally forgetting about Bro Mel's earlier counsel. I thought that "if it's a two-way street, I'd use it." So OK, cool, and so that night my eyes were closed and I was searching about and I found something. No idea what this was. It was like a TV show illustrating how the brain functions and I could see synapses firing and connections being made, and this couldn't be me. It had to have been one of them! After all, I knew I couldn't mentally restructure myself, my thoughts couldn't alter my very own flesh. So OK, once again, cool, I looked this scene over then imagined seeing my finger in it, and then, I saw my finger, it was just there. So I thought I'd just stick this finger in and stir things up a bit - just a wee bit. Next day, I heard this spirit grumbling and complaining. "Man what is going on here? I'm a spirit, and I itch; what is this?" "This is awful, but this is crazy this can't be happening to me. We're immune to any illness or any of the nasty things done to you. What the heck, Paul?"

At first this seemed like terrific fun, then, well, not so much. After a time or two of this, I got to thinking this wasn't right. It didn't feel right; I was using this without much thought (and that always got me in trouble before.) Scripture teaches that God made everything; that's really everything, even including the things that were likely to be used for evil. And I ought not to do the same things they did, they had been good creations originally but not now. So, I determined to be kind to the things and hope that was correct. After all, that was operating in the opposite spirit, wasn't it? Something that I'd strayed from in my irritation!

A few nights later, I was about to fall asleep when I got a picture of a demon lying down to sleep, and I thought to cover the thing with my blanket. Like when I used my finger earlier, it was an image in my imagination that I was working with, and it came up in a fury! But I had treated my enemy with compassion, and that was biblically correct, right? The demons retaliated by causing me to itch at night, really itch. And they would mess with my genitals and taunt me. I couldn't find the right demons to cast out, or get at them any faster, not then.

A Spiritual Warfare Ensemble

I wound up sleeping in itchy long johns, hoping to mask the demonic itching, wedged into the cushions on the living room couch with a towel between my legs. I had to do something to stop the itching and this lasted until I made better progress in casting them out. I still mentally flinch and get ticked when Christian leaders say, "don't worry about them demons son; they can't bother you." Church was starting to improve some; a few more folks were attending services and another church member, named Cindy Richards, sat down one Sunday and started helping me. Bro Mel told me, "She had suffered much over many years;" I liked her. She would sit down and look at me concentrate a moment and start to call out demons, and not unkindly. She informed them that it was time; they had to go now, and then cast them out; huh..? She saw the things; she said she saw them in silhouette. This was not Bro Mel's "in your face deliverance," - this was unique. On the occasions, she helped me; she would see them and maybe hear them too? Somehow, she had an understanding of what legal permissions they had going for them. Or, often, she'd discern that by conversation and confession.

Permission is required for them "to legally" occupy a person; they cannot just enter whoever and whenever they wanted to, there has to be an open door. Then, understanding how they got in she would cancel their permissions, casting them out in Jesus's name. This involved a lot of frank confessions and wide-open conversations, all done in public, shortly after services at church. This confession time, gave her an idea of what was going on with the things, and the Holy Spirit I soon realized, would give her their names. Incidentally, public confession is as old as the Christian Church itself, and good for the soul very powerful. She was really helpful, and lots of issues were covered in a relatively short time. She saw where spiritual connections were with the demonic, both from my life in Mercy Ships and my time living in other cultures. Curses were broken from different shamans, who were enemies from various ports, wanting to destroy the crew and Christian workers aboard the Anastasis. Curses were broken from meals taken with locals, where kitchen staff had cursed the foreigner's food.

The Resistance

And curses were broken from disgruntled patients from Mercy Ships; as no-one does everything well, every day, in everyone's eyes. Some folks were unhappy as the results didn't match their expectations, and in their pique, they didn't return to see what more could have been done; they just cursed. All my life, I had been such an open door for the demonic, the first demons hitting me (right at conception) had been wicked spirits whose function was to attract other evil spirits. I didn't get saved until I was thirty-nine years old, and didn't begin to understand what was what and how to defend myself until recently.

It still astonishes me that to be subject to such demonic difficulties as I'd withstood. All you have to do, IS TO BE BORN, such is life in our far fallen world.

And all through this mess, I was working or steadily job hunting. Many days, I'd apply over the Internet and interview at every opportunity. Usually, I was up against several hundred applicants or more for a given job. Then, on to an interview and then another. And I'd work my way down to the final interview with just a few opponents left. And always, someone had a tad better selection of qualifications and was way younger. No work, just looking for work, riding the Sporty and seeing Bro Mel, mostly weekly. I'd do spiritual warfare daily as inclined or by my schedule. That was my life, and I was determined to win. But all of this was taking its toll. I had more heart troubles, more operations and more stents implanted. I'd guess they were trying harder to kill me. A bout with lower colon difficulties, an exam and snip away and get the bleeding and about to become fully cancerous Polyps, out of there.

Problems with my teeth, groan, on and on, and on top of all of this, there was the constant drumbeat of lecture after lecture and trap after trap. It was just misery. There were spirits of death, spirits of inflammation and spirits of electrical disturbance to the heart, more cancer, lupus, insanity and confusion. Yup, don't worry about those demons, son. I know I'm not the only one out there. There's more to this whole thing than just this "tip of the iceberg" exposure of the demonic. This is also about obtaining a clear and clean conscience, and freedom to be what was intended for us. And right there, there is a leading reason they so oppose us. As then we can have a much greater impact within God's good Kingdom. Or in the world alongside our Lord's kingdom and amongst family and friends and strangers too. It's also, a great chance to jump-start our lives strengthening our relationship with Jesus Christ, all through this anti-demonic - pro-holiness, personal sanctification process. The rest of the satanic kingdom is not something I'm called to challenge, not by myself. But I got 'a get me free of this horrid mess!!

May God bless Cindy, Bro Mel, and Cindy's deliverance team. One day, I met with Cindy and her team in Boulder, Colorado. Cindy, Patty, and Tamara had often worked together, and it was exceptionally good. They ripped and slashed through those filthy things for five hours. That deliverance session brought me a greater ability to fight for myself; the advantage had slipped to the home team – Yeah Lord, Yes! Altogether things were slowly improving at All Nations Church and Deliverance Center, but all the while it was against stiff headwinds. I've heard Bro Mel say, "The devil doesn't care about all of the church's programs." What he cares about and will oppose is any "anointed undertaking by the church." I think he's right, especially about any anointing in deliverance! So, more and more, people are coming into this small church, but most don't stick around. For a while, there's staffer's coming from the area's largest church in Loveland. That church was starting a deliverance ministry. They'd come with notebooks in hand and I was one of the lessons, but I didn't care. I'd have stood on a street corner and been delivered over a bullhorn, if that's what it took to get meaningful help. Embarrassment be damned; I was going to win this fight! Bro Mel has a pastor's heart and will go about anywhere, anytime he can, and bring anyone he can to the Lord, and that's great. He'll also deliver anyone, anytime, with no qualifications. But that doesn't always work out so well. Some of the people that claimed salvation were weapons in the hands of the demons. These folks were so terribly demonized and so accustomed to being used by the demons that they were a threat to all. I'll talk some more on that later. Some others coming there were like me, wanting help in a hard-to-find area of ministry. They'd get help and soon be on their way. A few others were there as they found the church a good fit and felt they belonged and were needed.

The Resistance

These people were a real blessing. It's very pleasant to be working alongside the Lord. To see His power to save and redeem and heal at work, and Bro Mel wanted to see the folks helping each other, and that's an extremely healthy attitude. Me, I continued in my daily warfare and was getting delivered by Cindy and Bro Mel at about every opportunity. The demons were still lecturing, prodding, testing and messed with my emotions at every turn. I was fortunate that a couple from Austin Texas, the Joys, were super good long term friends. All through this, I'd been able to look to Rob for some "baseline" sanity help. What I meant by that was; when I was pondering if the blasted things were getting to me and I was going wacko. I could call and discuss things with someone that was not under such an assault. It's quite encouraging when someone can identify with you, and Rob is no virgin in this area. He'd been viciously attacked at times and understood from personal experience some of the nonsenses I've had to endure, but sometimes, well not so much. Rob was visiting in Fort Collins, and after helping him with some property maintenance we went to lunch. And as we were eating and discussing general stuff, Rob asked how the warfare was going. So to illustrate, I just starting reporting what I'd heard from the things as we sat there talking. At one point, Rob looked at me with suspicion and alarm and said "If I didn't know better, I'd think you are out of your mind!"

I'd tired of being "the guy with all the demons" and needing help from whoever will help, and wearied of my own work. I decided that it was time for me to record some of this stuff for others. There's just got to be something of value here for someone else. So I started typing out the commands I was using, then my thoughts, my reasoning's and some history about all this. And a bit later, I decided that I needed to write a pamphlet. Writing for people that needed help, and right now, for use at All Nations Church. I reasoned that the church could use such a handout. Especially when visitors asked how they might proceed after the realization that deliverance was real, and felt the need to investigate further. Boy, this was a tough undertaking and took a lot of revisions. The enemy did not want it done, not at all. And of course, as I was still heavily infested, they had a lot of power over me and continually assaulted my thoughts making it tougher to write. Eventually, I got it done and while doing this task, I discovered that my warfare was working well. But for a long time then, I hadn't understood the real extent of the enemy's assault on All Nations Church itself. Now that I've arrived at the far end of my story: I can see the intensity of the fight. But actually, so far in all this reporting, I've just been painting a picture of the blasted things, and of my lifelong battle for my mind and how that affected my soul. The reasons underlying my experiences are on display here and not too hard to fathom. The most difficult part overall was to realize that at this juncture. All of that work and the suffering and the torment and dedicated resistance were just learning experiences. It was a good start, but in no way were those methods developed so far, capable of fully delivering me; I was still stuck! It wasn't until my last season of "troubles" that I found what I needed to complete winning this fight. You see there was one giant overriding problem then, at All Nations Church. A women I'll call Jane; she was the point of the spear of the satanic kingdom's attack against that church.

It's hard to build a congregation when demons are attacking church members, they sure won't stick around. Jane was saved; she said by Bro Mel. And often, she was seen hitching a ride to Church with him. She's very easy to remember once you meet her as she's almost as wide as she is tall. And she would be a nice looking person, excepting that, of being so awfully overweight. Jane's also stooped, stooped from the hips and shoulders forward - an awkward picture. She is intelligent, extremely well educated, and incredibly demonized. And that's unlikely to change anytime soon, and that makes her terribly dangerous. Jane was a weapon the demons used to attack others, anyone vulnerable. She was an exceedingly angry person. I confronted her one morning at church, identifying her spirits for her, ones that had attacked me on many nights. Spirits that I knew were from her! Spirits of spousal abuse, man killing spirits, the spirits of rape, hatred, inflammation, death, rage and anger and insanity. She sat there nodding her head yes and acknowledging that those spirits were hers. I told her that she had to repent of these emotions and wrong attitudes and renounce those wicked spirits which were so active in her. She just had to. You see that without repentance, without denouncing and renouncing her demons; there was no way for her to be delivered from the demons and be healed. But she flat out refused!

Jane in her anger, her bitterness and refusal to forgive others was a spiritual open door for the demonic. Often admitting various spirits and getting a bit angrier with each. She would sleep soundly; everything was OK with her sleep. In the midst of her sleep though, the things would be very active, looking for an opportunity to attack, anyone and anywhere. I got to know this because those things often awakened me; I was a target. In defending myself, I would interrogate the spirits and find out they were hers and cast them away from me and to the pit. One day, Jane, quite haughtily told my deliverer friend Cindy that she was going to bring down the church. Jane was an enemy. But, she was not recognized as one for quite a while as she occasionally submitted to some deliverance, although she never initiated it. At times she did seem to want help. Sometimes, it appeared that Jane wanted to be helpful to others in the church, which might have been a ruse, maybe unknowingly. Whether she was aware of their tricks or not, I don't know. Sometimes the demons would supplant her, and they wouldn't show through they were in such control.

I'm probably going to embarrass myself a wee bit here. I'm sure some of you will wonder why I didn't recognize what was happening. Well, I did, but it took time. Originally there was scant opportunity for me to realize this, particularly when I was new to All Nations, Jane had already been there a while. Also, it's hard to understand just what's working against you, when a skilled enemy is hard at his task - a highly experienced and deceptive enemy. In a short while, I'm going to share about a deception that I got caught up in. I wasn't alone; there were thousands of others, and the instigator of the deception, for sure, did not want to want to hurt others! She was a hard working woman in a difficult ministry, a women who wanted to bless people and combat the enemy in new and powerful ways; new ways that were very effective. But, these new ways had a price tag attached, which I'm sure she has not yet fully realized. So, here I am in a deliverance church and practicing self-deliverance and slowly making headway. And it's increasingly paying off. I like the confirmation that speaks of. As I've rightfully observed that in the practice of deliverance, nothing can be accomplished in a person's own strength. The demons would delightedly mock you and roll on the ground in laughter.

And as I was evicting them, lots of them! I was gradually gaining greater knowledge, greater authority over the demonic, day by day and confrontation by confrontation. The Lord honor's his people's efforts to defend from and defeat this awful enemy, as His people, wholly, solely, rely on His Holy-Name, so cool. And yes, even if those attempts are rather clumsy at first! But still, there are life's practical things and there was no work in sight for me, no matter how prepared I was. I was still on the verge of retirement and now that I'd been out of work for a while, I was no longer current, great. I thought I'd have to demonstrate that I still had the knowledge to do the job! So I took some fresh networking certifications and passed comfortably, but I was still, just too old to get hired. The only places seriously wanting to talk with me were too far away. Commuting expenses and low wages there meant I'd be working for nothing and going backward, boo on this recession. So, its unemployment and that sometimes stops. That is until the Feds fund the next round of unemployment. My savings were getting thin so I started Social Security retirement benefits early. But that is too little to live on, and yes, the enemy's quite efficient at his work.

I used to have a bit of money, and at one time a secure retirement, but not now. And by conventional psychiatric standards, I was still mad as a hatter, but still quite sane; same old story. I knew what the voices were, but the shrinks they wouldn't believe me! Best of all was this, I was getting spiritually clean, well-scrubbed, despite all of the enemy's exertions against me. Some might say that's not much of a report card. But I was doing the grading, and the Holy Spirit is the final grader; He's solidly on my side. The Lord Jesus Christ, the true Holy Spirit, and my Heavenly Father, that's Jehovah God, and He's rooting for me and helping. It's mine to win. I've got to stay active no matter the cost, but I am tired. About a week later, I got an email from Betty, a friend of Lisa's Joys and an acquaintance of mine. In it, she recommended a book, Regions of Captivities by Ana Mendez Ferrell. Now, there's no way I'd recommend that book to anyone! Back then, I bought the book from Amazon and read it through. The story and the theory behind it were like this. Ana had a twin sister with deadly health issues in a Mexican hospital dying, a close sister.

The Resistance

Ana was praying, hard, trying to find something, anything to help her. She got personal revelation and started reading the Psalms and other scriptures. She noted that David and other biblical writers and prophets,' were speaking of what sounds like real places, locations in the regions of Hell. She figured if this was the right interpretation, and those places were as described that she needed to get to the bottom of this. She needed to see what could apply and so investigates; Ana's not bashful. Ana got further revelations that she took to some very popular and nationally known TV pastors, and they believed she was onto something. The method of this ministry went like this: through prayer and heaven's intervention, Ana got to accompany an angel to the "regions of Hell." She was escorted to destinations where pieces of her sister's soul had been stolen away from her, imprisoned by demons at seasons of stress in her sister's life. Huh…? Well, Brian Melvin, (way back on page 10 of Book One) told of his trip there, he'd actually been there, Hell that is. Then, I looked up the scriptures. And yup, I'd found the biblical texts she was referring to and it looked like accurate quotes to me.

It says just what she says it does, and so I gave Bro Mel a copy and waited on his opinion. It took a few weeks, and he'd no comment for me, outside of saying that: it's poorly written. And it sure was. And so, onward. While Ana's in the company of an angel, she journeyed through spooky looking, netherworld styled passageways and saw places of confinement, cells, chambers, pits, and alien landscapes. After arriving at one of the chambers. She found an image or piece of her sister's soul and brought it out of there. Along with her and her accompanying angel, returning to this world by retracing their route. Then, she sees this ethereal, insubstantial image of her sister merge with her sister's body. Who then recovered and was out of the hospital in short order. This manner of deliverance and healing sounded pretty wild. But, I wondered would it work for me? As so far, I could only follow the methods I'd learned, and they'd not freed me. No matter all the work and long hours I'd invested, all this time, treasure, and effort. Something's got to give!

There was a humongous problem here, and it was the primary reason I wasn't getting free; I keep combating Jane's junk. This is how I found it worked; there was a prince demon in Jane, say a spirit named Typhoid Mary. And this spirit had the task of spreading demons like the historical Typhoid Mary did, carrying and spreading that disease. Go to church and encounter Jane and these things were at you. It's like being downhill from loose gravel; you know some of its coming your way. As for the spirits themselves, I'll explain how that worked. One day after Church while fellowshipping I saw Jane, and her demons were manifesting. It was easy to spot in her. Her face went blank, her mouth shifted and her lips tightened into a straight line. She looked as though she was wearing a mask. I got distracted by someone, and Jane walked past and reached up to touch my shoulder. I realized she'd touched me, and I looked at her. Her head was down, and she was walking away from me and out the door; what the? Well, I had just down-sized from my house to a downtown Fort Collins "Senior Apartments" studio apartment. Well, Jane had tagged me with a spirit and that spirit was placed to locate me, once again, allowing the attacking spirits to resume the harassment.

Jane was cooperating with the demons so much so that they were controlling and supplanting her and doing their missions through her! They were driving her around like an old pickup truck like they had wanted to do to me! Some weeks later, Cindy and I were talking and this came out in our conversation. That's great I said then "it's no wonder I can't get rid of all the blasted harassment." So – Okay, to explain further: her filthy spirits were headed my way, a power demon in her, probably a prince demon (Typhoid Mary) connected with a power demon in me. The connection is called a "spirit tie." And a boatload of the things were then directed towards me. On their arrival, they assumed their places and roles against me led by the leadership hidden within and away from me. I couldn't find these spirit powers to cast them out as they were hidden away, working against me in league with "spirits of deception." Numerous demons were hiding, sheltering under the deceptive spirits covering. I couldn't get past these spirits because their precise function was to be busily deceiving me! Rats! What complete misery! It was all a demonic trap, this whole organization. This stronghold in me that was frustrating me. I just couldn't get much ahead back then; all

I could do was to cast them out at my best rate. It's no wonder my progress was so slow, way back then, argh, sigh.

I hated this; and thought, I've no options left, and I've got to try something different! I reread Ana's book and decided to give it a go. So OK, eyes closed and prayer accomplished. I asked the Lord Jesus Christ to please help me to work with His Holy Angels, and that I might employ these techniques to get to the root of the opposition. I let myself go and slowly relaxed and watched. And after a bit, clouds formed, a tunnel opened up, and I saw myself traveling along it. (This was a vision, it was something I saw and experienced in my mind's eye). I then came out and went past the clouds and saw a landscape opening up. There were some woods and a lake off to the left, a cabin in the foreground and to the right a small town. A mini New Jerusalem. The town's in the background, and I can travel there just by thinking. After a bit that fades and I wondered, what was all that? I read more from Ana's book. And soon realized that this is not at all like my "out of body trip" to "God's Holy Mountain," written of in Book One, Chapter 7. That trip was more tangible than my apartment: this experience was indistinct, fuzzy, and hard to see much in, most certainly a much lower quality experience. But, was it a valid spiritual experience? And if it were, how was I to get any help from all this? I figured I had to continue on this path, (for lack of an alternative) and hoped that should it prove out, over time, to be an invalid path. That Cindy or Bro Mel would see that, and I purposed to report to them as any opportunity allowed and keep at it until I could be sure, one way or another.

"Looking back, an Overview"

~~~

Deception is a hard place to be situated in. It's a tough neighborhood. Accepting it and continuing along with it (once discovered) could be somewhat comfortable. But it's the comfort of a slave, the personal experience of real helplessness. Jane is at that place; she won't even fight for her very soul. I've seen her when pastor's sermon confronted her with the knowledge of her sinfulness. She'd slip into abject despair. She understands her position, her peril, but still won't repent.

"Thoughts to take Away"

~~~

You can't be alone in your quest for sanctification, for the freedom you must obtain, striving to be the person God wants you to be. You must have help. It's what the body of Christ is for. Be forewarned be prepared and expect struggles. There are ebbs and flows in this battle. This is an ongoing continual war, and we're all stuck struggling along within it.

Chapter-Eleven

- The Deception -

So what can be the use of this, this seeing heavenly stuff? Well, I didn't know. I guessed I'd just have to continue on and see what might be of help. This haunting, this stinking oppression it just can't keep on; I was so sick of this. So it's off on another trip to the heavenlies and to the portal up there. I used the same procedure as I had earlier, (prayer, a comfortable recliner, no distractions etc.) And this crossing, this vision, it was about the same as the last the tunnel and all, only this time I encountered an angel. This angelic fellow, he looked pretty much as I supposed an angel would look. He was curious about me; we gazed at each other, and I said hello, how are ya` (just to break the ice). The angel was taller than I and quite stocky; he was gold-hued with some armoring and mighty wings. We stood there awhile getting acquainted chatting for a bit. Then, he grinned and placed a hand on my shoulder, and I got a better tour than I had on my own. I asked him about his wings, and he explained that this was a boundary style of vision.

"Kind of like an electronic interface, with images representing greater things and I would see him pretty much as I'd expect to." Also, that it was more about my expectations as this was a personal image, one that affected both his and my worlds. And it was wholly spiritual in nature and well outside the three dimensions of my world, length - X - width - X - height, that sort of thing. His name was AmoShah, and he would meet me whenever I choose to come up. OK cool I thought. So now I was a heavenly day tripper; no spaceship required. Eat your heart out Captain Kirk. But, can this thing come together for me as it did for Ana? There was a deliverance conference scheduled in Jacksonville, Florida, which I couldn't afford. But then, I couldn't afford more heart work or the ongoing insanity of this demonic harassment either. Should I go Lord? I talked with Rob and Lisa on the phone, and they thought this was worth going to. I wasn't so sure, not at this juncture; there's no way to know if this offered a solution? But, I had to do something, something that was a lot more useful, Boo.

I so was sick of barely surviving and of keeping my head just above water nearly drowning in demons. I've never been free from the demonic; I just didn't have any idea of how serious this could get! I had absolutely no inkling of the extent of it all; no idea, not at all, not until my Brother Walter's death. Lastly and most importantly, I believed the Lord wanted me to go, and that meant I was going to go. So, onward and upward, with my bags packed and tickets in hand. I'd got the airport shuttle, the flight schedules, and the directions to the meeting written down. I saved them in different places, just to be sure as I was expecting some opposition. It seemed to me that things from the Lord rarely went unopposed and sure enough. Later that night as I took to my bed a spirit hit me. It manifested right above me, saying: "Jane heard you were going for a trip, and I came by to wish you troubled sailing." I went right after the thing and cast it away, straight into the pit. Soon, it was to be followed by another, and another and another - all night long!

- This wasn't just a show of opposition; this was full-court-press opposition. When I finally arrived at the airport in Florida, my head was spinning so badly I could hardly walk. There's a whole long story to finding the conference as the demons had me so sleep deprived and confused. And at the airport I'd discovered I'd lost my directions and the convention address, everything I had written down. It was a good thing it was an easy run, a nice straight shot on the freeway to a well-marked exit and on to the convention center as I couldn't have found it otherwise. I finally arrived, checked in, booked a room and did succeed in getting some sleep, at long last, exhaustion can do that.

Next morning, I grabbed a quick bite, registered, and snagged a seat at the conference. The place was jumping; there was a worship leader from New Orleans, and he was more than a little enthusiastic and had a pretty decent band. There was solid Christian worship music, pulsing away, and the setting was well designed. Cool, nothing wrong there. There were about eight hundred people attending; it was exhilarating and such good fun. Ana and her troop arrived in formation like visiting Indian Pooh-Bahs' and took up reserved seats. Not so good I thought.

The Deception

A faint alarm bell going off, big church, elitist, "experts" variety of culture it was an insider's club, and I knew about clubs. So after a time of greeting and exhortation, Ana got in gear and had an illustration for us. She had a circle of chairs setup on stage and called for volunteers. OK I thought, there's a skit in the making, I like skits, cool. Volunteers came to the stage and sorted themselves out and Ana' took the first person to run to the stage, a gal, using her for a deliverance demo and seated her at the center. She went on to say that, in most deliverance ministries there's a problem. Delivers were doing their best. But because they were unaware of the revelation Ana was championing; they could not do a full deliverance; they were leaving the job incomplete. She illustrated this by having some individuals come into the circle as though they were demons and pretend to assault this gal. She then chased them all out as her technique was supposed to do. Next, she had the gal stand up, prayed for her and mentioned seeing a captivity in operation. She spoke of an angel and herself, approaching the place of this gal's spiritual imprisonment, then freeing her captured bit of soul from that place.

Lastly, she reported on seeing that stolen piece of the woman's soul returned and rejoined to her. The gal's mouth fell open and she appeared to be overwhelmed and startled by the deliverance. If this gal were a ringer she was a darned good one; and if this was a deception it was ably done. Then Ana attempted a mass deliverance for the audience. It felt like something had definitely been affected. And as the meeting broke for lunch, I went for a walk in the hopes that I'd actually been freed, but that wasn't the case. The real question was, was this worth looking at some more? Later that afternoon, Ana did an impartation, (installing some benefit from the Lord, some anointing.) The impartation occurred as she painted a verbal picture of a heavenly portal, a gateway. OK, I've been there and received that already I thought, remembering my trips. But then, another picture was about to come. In this one, there was a Judge in attendance in the portal one that can be available for a person's help. There was also, a set of counselors for questions and advice, curious eh? The conference ended late at night, and I didn't stick around for the last bits opting for some sleep.

A Spiritual Warfare Ensemble

I got a few hours before getting up for my red eye flight, and I felt better than I could remember. Boy I couldn't remember feeling any where's near this good, not in a very long while it was so refreshingly cool. And so sad that I had to go back home. So OK, sigh, it was a return to the Fort and as I approached Denver that superb feeling. Well, that wondrous sensation, it slowly dissipated and it was again, so sad! I caught the airport shuttle back north and a van to my apartment. And as I rode, all the goodness went away too and as I entered my place, I distinctly heard them. It was the same kind of demonic spirits, the same crew that had hit me the night before the flight and it was back to combat. There were so many times I seriously despised how the spirits from that woman keep finding and attacking me. I had to work extremely hard to keep forgiving her, over and over. And spent way too much effort into prying myself into a much better attitude, knowing I was liable to be seeing her at Church, this so, sucked and felt endless.

A word on that, all through this fight, every night I'd settle down for a time of worship and praise. I'd work on keeping my shopping list of needed items, out of play, and just try to review the day and be grateful for the good things. A funny thing happened in the midst of all this. When this first started I could hardly sing a note of song, but as all the warfare, the self-deliverance and the first hints of a coming freedom got accomplished. I discovered I could hit some true notes and kind of carry a tune. Neat, thanks Lord. As far as Jane was concerned I tried talking to Bro Mel about this situation; and he didn't seem to believe me. It must be my fault I thought, similar to past situations I've written about here. I'm not the well setup, handsome, college-grad type guy, I despise sniveling and downplay my difficulties often deferring to others, and I was a team player. And I tried hard, not to be the "squeaky wheel type" crying out for attention. But, I've often wondered, is that squeaky wheel type of person, is that the only way to get a response from others? Bro Mel just couldn't see it. But, there was a definite downside to ministering deliverance to the "anyone, anywhere, in any condition" style that he has. I understood his wanting to minister to all, but I also understand what I experienced then, and just wish we lived lives freer from our vicious deceptive enemy. The facts are: you cannot deliver a person against their will. You cannot free a person who has no forgiveness to others and who has anger and hatred in their heart. You just can't do it. God's word says, in Ephesians 4:32 you are to be "forgiving one another, just as God also forgave you in Christ. So to be qualified for deliverance, they must repent and seek forgiveness. I tried telling Bro Mel: that Jane was an enemy and should be told not to attend if she wasn't at church for deliverance. And she has to get her act together to be delivered. But he would not listen; it was my fault again, I'd guess, I sometimes don't present myself very well. But I couldn't remember when I (supposedly) had something so wrong, and events proved my point and anyone noticed? This situation with Jane felt just like the one with Larry the prosthetist. I saw the problems with him, but others in direct leadership over me couldn't, at least not until they were compelled to. I got saved at thirty-nine and haven't looked back; I wouldn't want to be a screw-up again, not again. I wouldn't go back there again, not for anything not even with my present troubles. Often, when Jane was at church I'd hear her spirits and feel them probing, hissing, and searching for open doors in me. "You've been working hard," they'd hiss as her serpents probed, trying to find any openings. Boy, I truly hated experiencing that!

So it was back to basics, once again. I began thinking I'd have to do more to help myself; it was a must, I had little choice. So I proposed to try this new "Ana style" approach some more, and give it a solid go. I hit the recliner, relaxed, and prayed for a bit and then lift off, and I was off. There was the cloud like earlier; next there was a kind of staging area and a set of armor to put on, cool. After that along came the tunnel, then through the tunnel and then there was a portal and my angel, waiting. AmoShah grabbed a hold, latching on at my shoulder and we hopped down to meet the Judge. The Judge was busy, writing in something but took a break, and we met formally. I told him about my need to get free from the attacking demons and to get to the root of things. He nodded and said "be right back," and he was off to talk to his boss. Soon enough, he was back again and with a scroll. It was maybe ten inches long and fairly thick; he handed it to me and explained, that scroll is my seal of protection and permissions, "don't lose it." AmoShah and I headed down some shadowy cobblestone staircases and long irregular corridors, heading deeper.

We passed through grayish shafts, sometimes lined with ancient looking dismal cells. There were flashes of light here and there, but otherwise it was a place of dark shadows. It was dark and dank looking. I was glad I couldn't smell anything. Finally, we arrived at a door with a plaque over it. The plaque read "Fear," and I gave it a yank and pulled it fully open. Inside it was all shadows, gloom, and darkness. But there was a young me in there, chained to the wall. "That's just not good" I thought then. At first I couldn't break the chain pinning the child to the wall, and then I thought of the "permissions in the scroll." I used the scroll to smack and break the chains and that worked great. So I grabbed the kid by the hand and headed back to the portal with AmoShah. Meantime the youngster had grown to full size over the course of the return. And when we get back to the portal, he took off. Off he went as AmoShah said, to heal and rest. I didn't see any of this merging, like in the book or at the conference. But everything in this spiritual warfare is so individual, and so custom tailored mostly affecting a person in their weaknesses, so who can tell?

Me, I was quietly, desperately, trying to feel and figure my way through all of this. Then, I realized what this trip was about. When I was little, my family lived in a huge old barn of a house. This place was three floors in all, the top two floors with seven large rooms each. The lowest level had two vacant stores and had been a neighborhood grocery in Brooklyn, New York, long ago. Behind the storefronts were the buildings side doors and staircase to the upper floors. Underneath was the basement that had been a stable, predating the automobile. Me, I was a natural explorer, but I was scared by the darkness at the back of the staircase which overshadowed the cellar door. I was afraid of going back there, really scared. But eventually, I got past my dread and went downstairs to the basement to find a bunch of old stuff to explore. The fright of a child's imagination had been manipulated by the demons that saw an opportunity. Filthy things they stuck me with a hot button of fear.

OK, is this Ana thing for real? If my vivid "out of the body," "God's Holy Mountain" had been a ten. Then this Ana style was just a three or two maybe even less. It's hard to know most of the time, and this is all so vague emotionless and convoluted. What's being affected?

The Deception

Not so much. It's the usual daily warfare. I still can't stop their endless talking plotting and lecturing. Sleep is still a crapshoot, yet, despite all these "headwinds," I'm pleasant enough to be around as I made some new friends and acquaintances, I've handled this well.

But by any conventional standards I'm still mad as a hatter. Yet I'm still me, and this will be defeated; yes Lord.

At that time, I made a discovery; I found that I could recognize the things (their voices) in some other demonized people. It was very similar to my friend Cindy, who would discern the spirits and see them in silhouette. What I discovered was, if I concentrated, looking to a person purposing to find what I might hear, I'd encounter first some resistance and then, "who's that?" from a demon. Then, "hey you can't do this; who are you?" And from this starting point on, I began using my pamphlet style of deliverance on them and tossed the things out. I'd sit down, begin with a blank sheet of paper and record the demons names. Then I'd interrogate them further to discover their functions and tear down any structures I found. I was adept at it and getting better. It struck me then that sometimes I must be using the enemy's tools and methods against them. But principally, no matter the method. It was the power of the Holy Spirit, overruling those demons and compelling their obedience; that's the Holy Spirit's power - that's what did the kicking out - not me. Please realize this in deliverance, nothing can be accomplished in a person's own strength. You must know who you are in Christ and authority comes with usage. This new ability I'd discovered. This was pretty wild, and I thought I'd better keep all this straight, somehow. These were strange waters to navigate and there were no charts, none at all. I periodically kept in touch with Rob and Lisa and they still felt Ana's methods had some weight to them and would be a valuable help, me, I wasn't so sure. All I could do was outline what I experienced to Bro Mel and Cindy, hoping they would alert me should they perceive this was some kind of demonic trick. A few weeks later Rob suggested that I come down to Austin to see if I could deliver him from any demons. Why not? I thought; I could use a break. Later he and I were sitting at his dining room table and we quickly got to business.

I'd concentrate and recognize a kind of wall, focus a bit more and get past it, and then I heard a spirit in Rob say, "Who are you? Bro Mel I've heard of! But who are you, his sorcerer's apprentice? Oops. A poor choice of words there," said the demon in Rob, and it was. And we're off to the races. I'd seen this before. Occasionally, when I connected with a spirit it scowled and was nasty. Then, it would quickly take on a lighter and milder tone. My time spent trying to be biblically correct and just, and just business-like, had paid off. The Holy Spirit set limits on them, and they set their personal resistance based on how they've been treated by you. If you rant at them, you're empowering them. Earlier, I had foolishly started doing things "their way," and rummaged around in the mind of one of the spirits. After realizing that was a mistake, I stopped doing that and started doing things biblically. I did this by showing kindness to my enemies (they did hate it when I did that) and I got punished for it by intense itching. The heart of the matter is this, they're also creations of God, and should have a modicum of respect because of that, but just a modicum no more.

I also noted that I'd said nothing about Bro Mel during my deliverance session with Rob. It seemed the demons communicated instantly as they purposed to work together. Now back to the deliverance with Rob. So, I've got this one communicating, and he's my first target. Out comes the scratch paper and on with questions like. What's your name spirit, what's your function; when did you enter? Who do you report to? And then on with Rob's deliverance. After a while, I identified what had to be a structure and found the leaders, the "power demons," and cast them out. I started with the highest ranking one's going after all to be found. Some hours later Rob and I were whipped. Deliverance's being done that way, this manner of interrogation and listing of the demons details by name, function, sometimes its history is exhausting work. Shortly after, Rob went to bed. The next evening after work, Rob said, "that was the best deliverance I've ever encountered!" I also delivered some folks over the phone and was pretty good at it. Altogether, I surmised this was structural anti-stronghold work; it was just one approach, just one piece of the puzzle.

The Deception

But it was the same deal, the same limited results, and there were demons left in residence after the deliverance, like over the last few years for me! This is all well and good this deliverance-in-detail, but how do you clean out all of those things? What are the last bits and pieces of this puzzle? How are we to get totally free of them? What I am talking about here, is how do you achieve complete sanctification from them? What're the facts? The nuts and bolts of sanctification? I prayed about this and tried internet searches and found precious little about the subject. There were a few references to sanctification in my Mercy Ships DTS, but that was of little help now, memory only serves so far. The best I could come up with was the books I was already using, especially "Soul Ties and Legal Ground" and "Prayers that Route Demons" as listed in the "End Notes." I used them one after the other, over and over again. Altogether, it wasn't too hard to tell when I was making headway; as these books were organized topically. So in my readings, I'd gradually clean out a topic, a subject by commanding prayer then continue on from there. As an example, when a deliverer casts out a spirit, different people react in differing ways. Many people expel the things by busily burping and yawning. Myself, I became an expert at burping. It seems the things could be located about anywhere, and different folks physically expel them in various ways, most often from the belly. It's entirely individual. Me, I'd start strongly then eventually lose the compulsion for burping, I'd slow down and then I'd finally stop burping at all. Yup, I knew then I'd hit on empty in a particular subject and just realized in my heart that I'd achieved freedom in that particular area.

One evening while I was rummaging around the Internet, I checked out Ana's website and got a terrific find. I obtained a copy of her new book entitled *"Iniquity-the major hindrance to seeing God's glory manifested in your life."* I skimmed through it and found it to be excellent (she must have gotten a ghost writer). As was typical of me, I read and re-read it over and over and put it to work. It seemed to me that this might be a useful approach to finding my spiritual roots and the blockages to my sanctification. Iniquities are the sins of our antecedents, those people who hated God and sinned. These sins by definition were unconfessed and unforgiven and were passed on in the bloodline by demons, and I believe, often by demon aggravated disease and an altered DNA.

And worst of all (these familiar spirits) they hit you from right at the moment of conception! After rereading her book several times. I came to the conclusion that the process she illustrated was intended for those who did not hear the demons and weren't so deep in combat, not like I was. So I decided to try a different approach. I'd go to prayer, asking the Holy Spirit to show me my antecedents and to give me an understanding of their sins, their iniquities, and what they were all about. Then I asked to be shown how to deal with them, and it worked. I got mental pictures and even images of distant relatives, some ancient, with an understanding of what was happening and to whom. I also had an understanding of how to pray about it. I asked the Lord Jesus Christ, to please come between me and the sins of my forebears. To destroy all curses and to please forgive and destroy these particular iniquities - the one's I'd just been shown and their associated demons too. I had to revisit some areas over and again, but the pattern was established. And after a while I got a better understanding of the nature of the iniquities and the folks that committed them and sometimes why. A few weeks of this and those areas were cleaned out, really well.

In the meantime I was continuing with the captivities. I would make trips to distant places accompanied by AmoShah and sometimes whole squads of Angels. Sometimes they would break off; I thought for combat with the demons. Angels make short work of demons but occasionally get hurt, but then they recover quite quickly. On one trip deep down somewhere, I entered the cell where AmoShah had lead, looking for something that would apply to me. My parents and brother, they had captivities there too; they were chained to a wall on my right and were yelling, "Go Paul, Go!" I was getting cheered on! I grabbed a small child that had to be a part of me; sure looked like it. I reversed course and headed back to the portal with AmoShah and let him loose, like before, a similar deal. On thinking about all these trips, my interviews with the Judge, and counselors that were introduced along with the Judge at the second "Ana conference." And these counselors who sometimes had no council, saying they'd get back to me and didn't. I had to wonder what was happening here; could this be true?

The Deception

Sometimes, I felt like the night's activities had set me free in a particular area, for instance, fear of man, that's no longer a problem after a night's session. Then, the proof of the pudding happened. An acquaintance from my time serving in Mercy Ships came by, hoping for deliverance at my Church. This man stayed in my apartment and spent all his time on the web or asking me question after question. He was a bit of a nuisance and pretty infested. I wondered if he would deal with it. So, I was in my bedroom that night, and he was situated elsewhere, and it was off to the heavenlies to see what would happen. Later that night, I found myself at a cell with a plaque that read "Transfer Point." What's this I wondered? I entered, and the cell door slammed shut behind me. That's not so good. So, I used the scroll to blow the door off its hinges, propped it up in the hallway and hopped back in, and looking around I saw my brother and me chained together to the wall. And thought, aha, that's right, "Transfer Point" that was the name over the cell I'd entered. And that's how they invaded me! I bet that's how I addressed the spirits in others. OK, I used the scroll to shatter the chains freeing me, and up and off to the portal we went with AmoShah. The next day, my guest and I were talking and I tried to deliver him same style as I did with Rob and some others, nope, nada, nothing. That kind of addressing the spirits in others, then sorting them out and then casting them out no longer worked. This Ana's "Regions of Captivity" style deliverance ministry has aspects that are valid and it does affect my reality, oh good. Nah rats, nope, sigh, I could still hear the things railing at me!

This spiritual warfare is strange stuff; one of the most annoying and trying things was the occasional ambush from Jane's junk. Remember I mentioned this connection with a coven? Well, that was backed up by the local territorial spirits. I would not want to mess with these things; they're part of the structure that Lucifer uses to manage his domain, this entire world. There are differing levels of spiritual warfare; the higher ranking ones are for Christian Communities working together to tackle, working over time and using discipline and in-depth biblical knowledge. That's a much higher level challenge, we individuals; we deal with the more minor spirits. There's a principle to remember here. All Christians have the right, make that the duty to protect themselves, their families and those needing or asking for their help.

A Spiritual Warfare Ensemble

In addition, those in church leadership have a responsibility to guard against the enemy's efforts against the Body of Christ under their authority. Lucifer is the ruler of this world; his kingdom is the satanic one, and it has its legal limits and its organizations and is not someplace we are authorized to just "mess with." No matter how much we may hate and despise those things and want to combat them. We are not authorized just to go about, aggressively demon hunting. If you feel that the Lord Jesus is telling you to get after them, those high ranking spirits in the heavenlies and someone quite knowledgeable, someone you are accountable to can confirm it, by all means. But. Consider the Apostle Paul's trials, the stoning's and floggings and shipwrecks. He didn't command the wind and waves! He didn't make war on the territorial spirits to prevent demonic attacks against himself. Yet he would most assuredly cast out an annoying spirit to defend himself and his ministry. Almost always when I get attacked now, it's because Jane's junk has instigated it, and I'm defending myself. And if I get a chance to I will answer, strongly. God has not given me a spirit of fear, but a spirit of love and joy and a sound mind and I am God's child. I'm an adopted son of God and won't be bullied, not if I can help it. Here's an example.

- One night, I was approaching sleep and started dreaming: I saw myself wearing a pith helmet and shorts in a jungle setting. There were palm trees, tropical ferns, and leafy plants galore. I had my magnifying glass out (just like Sherlock Holmes), and I was bent over trying to investigate something. It was an "invisible" stepped pyramid; like one of those Aztec things, (this was a dream, right?) except the pyramid, it was invisible. So, I scooped up sand and dirt and threw it on it and got an idea of the size of it, and it was growing. I had to step back; it kept growing. Then I am shoved out of my bed and onto the floor, what the...? I staggered up, and groggily wandered to the couch in the next room to continue in sleep, and sat bolt upright on arrival! What the...? I ran back to the bedroom to check the bed, and of course, found nothing. I thought I heard chuckling; it was more like being aware of chuckling. About six months later, I was facing down, catnapping on the couch, and I felt myself being pinned to it. I couldn't move, rats. I started calling out, "Jesus, Jesus, Jesus!" And rolled over, against stiff resistance and commanded, "Who are you? What's your name?" The thing told me its name, and said it was the spirit that staged the Aztec temple and asked how I liked that? Oh, yeah! I didn't

110

give it a chance to slip away, I immediately commanded, "In the name of the Lord Jesus Christ, I cast you away and into the pit of Hell." And pop, it was gone. Got ya.

"Looking back, an Overview"

≈≈

I remember writing earlier, how these were "uncharted waters" needing to be traversed. I only hope that by my being open and honest about all these things, you will see into my failings and confused responses and realize something. That all the while as I've been combating the demonic spirits. I've been doing it while still under their varied influences. It's been a hit or miss and necessary learning experience, and on my own I'd have certainly been destroyed. It's been the indwelling of the Holy Spirit which has allowed me to make the progress I have.

These spiritual interlopers need to be opposed, and cast out. The Pastor Jenkins's deliverance script offered at the conclusion of this book will reduce a lot of the need for any added charting. It's such a comprehensive, well organized, sharp edged tool, it cuts deftly into the ranks of the demonic oppressors. It bypasses their defenses and eliminates their options. They have no choice and must comply; it's the Holy Spirit empowering the scripts commands, backing up the deliverer and enforcing God's sovereign rule.

"Thoughts to Take Away"

≈≈

I would not want to repeat this experience, no, not at all. But, I'm a better man for the winning of it.

≈≈≈

- Now comes the preservation of that Victory -

111

Chapter-Twelve

- The Beginning of the End -

So, this is still my everyday life, this haunting this harassment, and I'm still stuck with it. I didn't know then how much of an improvement had occurred but it was clearly better. I knew I'd made some headway as the harassment had slowed, and the spirits weren't so quick to mess with me. I clearly understood the need to keep working, forcefully keeping the pressure on the things. And by then my form of resistance had changed some; it was buttressed by "Anna style" now, and fairly often. The daily warfare schedule was down to a few hours in the evenings, and it was time for prayer and praise and the occasional trips to the "portal in the heavenlies." I asked questions of the Judge and learned prayers for different situations and they worked. I told him about Jane and asked for his advice, and like My Pastor Bro Mel. He didn't seem to believe me? "He said - she said; he'll check." Off he went and in a bit, he returned to his bench and said, she's a real problem and will have to be dealt with, piecemeal, progressively and over time. That's great I thought then, but what does that actually mean?

It's also a real problem, this whole visionary experience, Ana style. Sometimes it's right on the money, and sometimes just suspicious. I often have to wonder how much demonic interference I experienced, and what the actual extent of it all was? Are my personal demons blocking and adjusting things to suit themselves, which was an exquisite question at that time. It was just another one of the odd puzzles of this whole being haunted thing, and it kept getting thicker. Meanwhile, I'd been pursuing sanctification and that was coming along nicely. God is gracious and the Holy Spirit was ready to help. The Iniquities had long been dealt with; yes, Lord! And the curses, spirit-ties and general family stuff had been well addressed by using the two books, *Soul Ties and Legal Ground*, and, *Prayers that Route Demons*. I'd re-read them over-and-over, praying through the book's prayers and commands aloud until I sensed no response from the wicked spirits.

A Spiritual Warfare Ensemble

I was still doing my daily scheduled warfare, using the form I wrote of in my pamphlets (let's continue to call that: deliverance-in-detail) at least several hours a day.

An explanation seems in order here. The process of deliverance used by Bro Mel and Cindy, they believed is entirely a product of the Holy Spirit, and I agree, in principle. I also recognize that their experience and outlook, and how they were feeling that day played a role too. Also, the spiritual condition of the person who's being ministered to, that too played a very influential part. So it's all mingled and not exclusively the Holy Spirit, Himself. Not all the time, so I don't think they'd disagree with that statement. Their concentration is on revelation, instinct, experience, the input of the Holy Spirit and what can be accomplished. That is until the deliverer was spent, or felt; there was no more to be accomplished that day. Sometimes that's a "stop" from the Lord; they'd say. Also, Bro Mel and Cindy are counselors, so that plays a substantial role in it as well. The Pastor Jenkins script which concludes this book is a well-organized and uniform approach. Which I believe; would serve well as a primary method, or as an adjunct and follow-on for any deliverance attempted. Because it goes places in pursuit of the demons that I had not experienced anywhere else.

This using it as an adjunct or a follow-up method of deliverance that's for someone who's well accustomed to their time-proven methods, like Bro Mel and Cindy, who often counsel and deliver. Other deliverance ministries, or persons wanting to self-deliver should just use the script as it's written. And that's because; it's so strongly focused on checking the spirits veracity while under interrogation. And doing this in a way that eliminates their options, as my pamphlets "deliverance in detail" style could not. The objection I've heard to this method of deliverance is that it will cleave the ranks of the demons so rapidly that the person will experience feeling as though they have lost themselves. That is, experiencing a sense of disassociation without all of their demons. I say cool, "Call them out," "Sort them out," "And cast the lot out." As I've learned that this lost feeling, is more of a consequence of the spirits operations when left within. Then an emotional product of someone whose life is no longer being bound and trespassed onto to the same familiar degree! It's been two years now since my open heart surgery, and I didn't do so well

114

until a few months ago. But now, it was absolutely worth it. It's that same way with deliverance, worth the discomfort and worth the efforts involved. Getting free quickly and proficiently is well worth any discomfort to me. How would you have liked living out this haunting of mine? I've genuinely loathed it!

Back to the story. So once again. I was considering this situation of mine, and thought about all the work and dedication it's taken to get this far and pondered; "has this become a fixation?" Had I made the switch from self-defense to making this coming freedom an idol in my life? On reflection, I thought no, no I wouldn't think so. I wasn't sure what the outcome would be, what full freedom would mean and what it will be like, but still it was war! I didn't choose it, and it's not going away - I've got to win it, and they'll be no excuses accepted, no settling for anything less than complete victory. At church I continued to intervene for its members and was active in prayer, and tried to use my Heavenly connections for helping others. One day, Cindy asked me for prayer; it seemed her teenage daughter had been missing a lot of high school, and that had been going on for a long time. Lately, it had been several weeks since she had the energy and clarity of mind to go to school. That night, when I remembered to pray for Cindy's daughter, I prayed, "Lord Jesus Christ, please intercede between Melissa and the attacking spirits sent from Jane and the attacking coven, and please destroy those spirits!" A word of explanation here: Cindy and I had talked earlier, she told me of some hard knocks in Melissa's life. But they had little impact on her education, and then things suddenly worsened. In the information technology field when a problem develops, the first thing you check for is what has changed. In discussing things with Cindy about her daughter's life, it seemed that her schooling abruptly went south when Jane first showed up. That didn't surprise me, first she caught some of life's hard knocks and then the open spiritual doors from those knocks, and then there's "Jane's junk!" A bit Later, I heard from Cindy that Melissa had returned to school, so cool. Others have used this intercessory manner of prayer, and it worked for them too. That prayer was from the Judge. Sometimes, I had my doubts about this whole heavenly portal shtick.

But when you're engaged in "working out your salvation with fear and trembling" as the word says you should do, and doing so while under the influence of spirits of deception. Well, it's extraordinarily tough to discern what is authentically of God. And what is a mixture of the heavenly and the demonic, and to what extent. I wasn't to learn until later that a mixture to any extent. Is entirely too much of a mixture and to just walk away. At Church, Bro Mel had finally realized the actuality of how dangerous Jane was and advised the congregation. He told them that she was an enemy and to be aware that when Jane was present they may be attacked. Huh? This simple warning was way too late; it was grossly overdue. I was seriously getting exasperated by this time! Why does this little Church have to get kicked around so hard? And then, more unwelcome news, one of my friendly fellow Church goers had died, at about fifty-two years old. He dropped dead shoveling snow, quietly succumbing to a heart attack, sadly, not an uncommon occurrence in snow country. I genuinely liked this man and this hurts, it runs in the family I'd heard. Then why was it that the cursing's in the family's bloodline had remained unbroken? He'd mentioned that early deaths were a long-running family curse!

I didn't get this, why this early death. I believed the strongest reasons for my survival are, number one. I've fought hard for it. And number two. It wasn't the Lord's will that the demons were to be the victors in my life, or anyone else's. But, had I succumbed to my fear and their torture and had not staunchly resisted them. Had I failed to fight the demons in any way I could think of. I'm pretty sure they'd have killed me. If that had happened, then the Lord would have lost any opportunity for being such a champion as I desperately needed. Or, I could have left it all to Bro Mel and Cindy's deliverance efforts, or tried it "man's way," with the psychiatric doctors and I knew what that meant. Bro Mel had admitted he'd no idea of how to proceed; Cindy had her troubles and was overworked as it was. Leaving this resistance of mine to them is not an option! It's me, the Holy Spirit and the "Body of Christ;" there has to be someone, some brother or sister somewhere who can help me get completely free. And this is what hurts, as I've survived this battle against the demonic, why not my friend who'd died?

The beginning of the End

Shortly after, it was a Wednesday evening bible study at church, and a ratty looking little Toyota pickup with a camper shell on it and a cracked windshield pulled up in front of the church. The driver laboriously, sluggishly, climbed out of this poor and used up truck joined by his wife; he was on two canes and looked like a garden gnome. They were unkempt, frumpy, and appeared like travelers sleeping rough on a long disused road. They came into the church, and as things commenced in the study the man started talking, incessantly talking. He took over the study with his utterings; no-one else had a chance to speak. I thought at the time; this is someone remarkable; we need to pay attention, obviously, (please forgive the sarcasm, but really.) He related that he was a Messianic Jew, a genius (they both were) and a spiritual warrior and slayer of many witches. He went on to relate that he's so special that he's accustomed to being tossed out of church's for disrupting meetings like he was doing then. I just had to groan, oh no, Jane's not been attending church here for a good while now and here's her replacement! Aw, crap!

So Joe and his lovely wife took center stage and started telling their stories, stories that were a mixture of jumbled disjointed personal history, their so-called ministry, and utter nonsense. After a while it becomes apparent that this couple is deluded and probably certifiable, most certainly the man, and I ought to know! And Joe kept rattling on, intensely speaking of the wonders of his peculiar life, Cindy looks as though she would like to leave town, about then. Bro Mel became quite interested, and more rattling on from Joe, and it was getting late. Being in a deliverance Church has its downsides, really! So, Bro Mel asks Joe about his salvation, and what Joe said was so bizarre and nasty, that this ordained, seminary educated, failed Baptist minister had to be in the pay of the enemy. Bro Mel looked the man full in the face and discernment kicked in, and he realized the guy was a warlock, and he was. I got back to the house late that night to get roundly attacked by spirits from Joe, great, sigh. Meanwhile, there's another Deliverance Conference from Ana's Voice of the Light Ministry; I've read her book on Communion, and it's quite good and put it into practice.

The books main point is first through fourth century Christian's, had practiced communion as a regular part of their daily life and community. After reading that, I often added communion to my nightly prayer and praise sessions and knew real benefits. Aha, I thought at the time. Another weapon, another tool for my anti-demon tool belt, cool. Cindy failed to find any fault with what I have experienced in the heavenlies, and I still saw Bro Mel for a weekly report. There are still suspicious things about this whole procedure, but nothing I can put my finger on and say, this is a show stopper. I voiced my concerns with AmoShah one night, and he replied by stating, "If I should find something that you were explicitly told to be false, walk away and don't come back," and I agreed. And so, it's off to Chicago, to the "Ana conference" and this time there's little demonic resistance, nice. There were about a thousand people there. The conference hall was a large rectangle; the stage centered and at the back, an awkward shape for what they did there, and the whole presentation was affected. Friends attending with me walked out and took long breaks as the sound was so frightfully bad. But the impartation was good (Wiktionary: impartation - To communicate the knowledge of), and I had a little better experience with the heavenlies, though not much. The conference had its high points, but things had not improved much for me. Since I still had no alternative, I decided I just needed to keep on, keeping on. I was still getting kicked around some, and then, then there was an aligning of spirits from Joe and Jane with a local coven, and that got promptly, speedily dealt with. (I used the same style of prayer spoken of earlier, asking the Lord Jesus Christ to intercede for me against those enemies attacking from outside me.) Thank you, Lord!

A word of explanation here. One of the things I've noticed in this Christian walk of mine is that the Lord does, indeed, intercede for us. He is Sovereign and can do whatever He wishes and, sometimes, will act for us. But this is far from an automatic; I'll ask for whatever I want, and the Lord will provide, of course not. When I've seen His hand involved in my life, it's at times when I've worked at following the calling I've been given. Invested in that calling and used my brain and what talents I have. I'd engaged and worked hard and finally gotten where things are beyond me. At that point, I would often see the Lord's direct encouragement and provision and know that extraordinary realization. That, hey. "The Creator God, the Lord of the Universe," has just moved on my behalf! It's similar in deliverance ministry; nothing could be accomplished in a person's own strength; the demons would delightedly mock you and roll on the ground in laughter. You have to go to work, and then the Holy Spirit will be the power you require. Overall, throughout all this, I've done my best to gain the knowledge and exercise the authority that the Lord has provided. I've worked with the Body of Christ, prayed, and genuinely loved and praised this mighty God of ours trying to do things His way. It's a real shame I can't do better at this; I'm stuck feeling my way through all of this! But my faith remains firmly, entirely, steadfastly in Him.

Bad news, once again, with my usual spotty spiritual batting average I swung and missed. I was deeply asleep and in the middle of the night startled awake. In my mind I clearly heard, "LOOK OUT!" And AmoShah was yelling at me. A Spirit from Joe was trying something so vile, so horrible that I had to be awoken by him. I had to be informed, NOW, AmoShah said. A master spirit or power spirit or something wickedly powerful, working with Joe's demons, has brought to birth a "spiritual daughter - of mine?" A - What…? A spirit baby; huh what the…? This would be a spirit-child birthed from my old biker days. Some sin, some raunchy event way back then, and the demons were to use this little "spirit-child" just to torture her, to torture me! If you have ever had a dream state where the reality is so confused, you think the dream is real but it wasn't, or is it, what the…? This was one of those times. What a mess my head just ached, I was swimming in confusion and dismay, huh great, what a gift from my new non-friend Joe, I thought.

This episode in hindsight was a combined assault, they'd staged an incoherent dream sequence in combination with palpable tension and mental confusion and deep sleep interruption. All this to introduce a new character, perhaps a clone, reproducing the Angel AmoShah. Someone to aid them in their earthly demonic deceptions. Looking back from my current demon free state, it seems that such a ploy wouldn't easily pass. But, again, when you're stuck being under the influence of deceptive spirits, it's terribly difficult to judge things correctly. Expecting people struggling against the demonic to accurately assess their situation is precarious. Even people without any apparent demonic interference can often be in denial or an avoidance mode. And they're just not seeing clearly enough to see how things are, it's a beam in the eye as illustrated so very ably by Jesus.

After Joe attended church and hung around Bro Mel's barbecue restaurant for a few weeks, Bro. Mel led Joe to the Lord, and it seemed as though he'd gotten genuinely saved, OK cool, I thought. The guy would show up at church and express repentance; he'd start confessing things and then quickly slowed down. So some others and I would chime in with places and people he'd spoken bitterly of, naming them for him to repent of. These were people that he had referred to in his rants, people he'd cursed! (And then did nothing to cancel those curses?) But who could tell where his heart truly was? Shortly after this the guy left to try to find work, bye-bye Joe, glad to see you go Joe, really! The harassment from him stopped, and I hadn't heard much from Jane lately. So this was much better, sigh, now if I could just get rid of the indwelling, interloping demons still about. The deception that began there with that shout from AmoShah lasted for some months. I'm sorry to say that my talks with my pastor or Cindy didn't alert them or me that this was going to be a serious problem. I thought there was an odd, strange blend in play then and that there was quite likely a mixture of the demonic and the heavenly, but where could it be and to what extent? One of the writers I'd read and whose book I'd employed in destroying my spirit ties, openly stated there was something of that mix in her life. I hardly knew of any active Christians where after I got to know them pretty well. I couldn't see some hint of that demonic element, in play, to some extent and in some manner. It was a rarity however, when negative symptoms were identified as having the possibility of being linked to the demonic. And even rarer that after being identified, that they were effectively diagnosed and treated by real deliverance. What do I mean by real? What the first couple that attempted a deliverance for me did, that was not real. It had little or no effect. It seemed like it was more along the lines of wishful thinking for the deliverers involved.

The beginning of the End

(I wrote about these folks early in Chapter Eight.) The pamphlet's I wrote, those were almost real, (you can find them at the back of this volume) but sadly they could not get the job done, not entirely.

What I am going to show you in a short while is the realest and most practical deliverance approach that I've found; it worked remarkably well for me. Had I known earlier about this deliverance method, I firmly believe my infestation could have been over in some weeks or months, rather than some years. Jane would have had a lot less impact as open doors would have been shut and exploring Ana's "captivities" would not have been required. But there is something troubling about that statement this one I just made. As I was going far out on a limb, trying to get to the roots of things, trying to get totally rid of the demons. I was also digging deep within myself, working hard to deal with any unconfessed, any unremembered, any unrealized sin. Anything at all not of the Lord, I wanted it out of my life. And I'd have hated to have missed this good and Godly quest. You see at that same time I was working on self-deliverance, I was also working full time to discover and practice the liberating process of sanctification, powerfully enhancing my anti-demon crusade. Without that anti-demonic impetus, my immediate and urgent need for freedom, the determination the need and craving for holiness might not have been there, and I treasure what progress I've made in sanctification. At the beginning of Book One I provided some scriptures that were crucial to my way of thinking. They exemplified my approach to my miserable situation. Here they are again (the underlining is mine).

2 Timothy 2:21 HCSB - 21 - So if anyone purifies himself from anything dishonorable, he will be a special instrument, set apart, useful to the Master, prepared for every good work

Hebrews 10:14 HCSB - 14 - For by a single offering he has perfected for all time those who are being sanctified.

Romans 12:1-2 HCSB - 1 - Therefore, brothers, by the mercies of God, I urge you to present your bodies as a living sacrifice, holy and pleasing to God; this is your spiritual worship. 2 - Do not be conformed to this age, but be transformed

121

by the renewing of your mind so that you may discern what is the good, pleasing, and perfect will of God.

These and other scriptures spoke to me of my desire; my need to clean up this life I'd lead. No matter what the cause of the events was, and where the influences came from, I was the one responsible. And when thinking on the subject of sanctification I remembered a teaching from my Mercy Ships DTS. It was about the idols in a person's life. I got to thinking about those idols and started to pray, and while in that prayerful mode. A mode that had morphed into an exploration of my personality and my character, composed of those forms, those styles of thinking, personality traits and personal characteristics I had come to revere. I thought about the idol of self, and the idols of my opinions, my rights and quirky individuality. I was thoroughly examining my personal qualities and looking to see if there were any gods that I'd built or allowed, idols to repent of and break. Soon enough, late one night the Holy Spirit showed me different images. In my mind's eye, I saw and knew what my idols were, and understood their very natures too! I was to reject, renounce and denounce all those things, one after the other.

Wow, this was terrific and then, after asking for forgiveness and the destruction of those idols in my life. Then they gradually crumbled away to dust. This was quite a show; it took a while to review and understand what I was seeing. I was engaged in doing this work for most of two nights, right in the depths of the night. So much for those idols; thank you Lord Jesus. I think that tearing down of idols was a genuinely valid process, a piece of the puzzle that contributes to a person's sanctification. Once started on this sanctification path, that quest had to be stuck to, no matter the demons continuous lectures and accusations and distractions. On another night, the Holy Spirit trumped that idol experience. I was about to get lost in sleep when I saw me as a young man. And in a scene well remembered one which I had blown, pretty badly. The Holy Spirit was to show me the scene, the time of my life, places and people and gave me a clear understanding of the event and the sin committed. Then, I repented, renounced and denounced those sins, asking for forgiveness and remittance, and then for the healing of any scars or damages to my soul from the consequences of that sin. The Holy Spirit brought to my mind scenes from my early life, from schools I attended, events and places where I had been, continuing until I was about four years of age and even then rebellious. And on one occasion, a demon trotted out and admitted that the particular sin I had seen was entirely of its construction. And that he was told by the Holy Spirit to take responsibility and admit the trapping and go straight into the pit. Cool. I would not have recalled any of those sins, not the dates, the places, the circumstances, the people or issues involved. Not like I had been shown, not on my own not at all. Sanctification is exceedingly neat! One last example from earlier, when the Holy Spirit was showing me the people involved in my family tree while working through the iniquities. I saw some medieval knight, who was in my family genealogy. My favorite Aunt knew about these antecedents. She had some antiques, some old records and mementos from former military officers, and from way back when, a Black Knight of Schleswig-Holstein or some such place. The Holy Spirit showed me that this knight was the primary source of all the iniquities I had gotten slammed with. I saw the circumstances of the sins in my forebear's lives and knew enough to ask for forgiveness, and to take personal responsibility for them. Thereby putting a halt to their chains of consequences, reconciling them thru Christ.

Then, asking the Lord Jesus to intercede between me and them and the results from their sin, asking Jesus to please forgive all those iniquities and destroy any demons associated with them! Yes, Lord! It took a while to find all that was there and when completed that was that. Nothing more to do in that area and nothing for the enemy to take advantage of. Think about it for a moment, we're heir to very many blessings from uncounted others just in everyday life. The balance to that is, in our bloodlines and our family trees, we're heir to our unrepentant forefather's sins, and the consequences of their sins, their iniquities. Lastly, I can imagine someone reading this and thinking, "What about Jesus death on the cross, didn't that one-time sacrifice cover all of our sins?" When Jesus suffered and died for us, the body of Christ, that's us, we believers. That event did indeed cover our sins; it removed the penalty "of the power of death" previously held over our heads. We received an "imputation" of righteousness, for as the Father commands, "We must be Holy as He is Holy," and we can't achieve that unaided. So, He does that for us, its undeserved merit and its grace. The power of sin previously resulting in death is broken, but the sin and its consequences remain. They remain active and in full effect, continuing *on until all the works involved in the nuts and bolts of the process of sanctification, are accomplished. That's when the sins the Holy Spirit reveals are confessed and repented of, and their consequences, including the demonic are addressed by the power of the Holy Spirit, Himself.*

So, continuing with my storyline. Altogether, I attended three of Ana's conferences, and at the last one I got an impartation that was illustrated as a portal for the Holy Spirit to use. He would be there whenever He chose to; He could be spoken with, interacted with. I was not comfortable with this and didn't do much with it. Fortunately, I was very preoccupied with getting free. Meanwhile, I was still looking for work, and I'd gotten a lead with a consulting shop in the Fort. And they had a contract coming up at an oil refinery in Wyoming. I made it past a few hundred other candidates, then a half dozen more, and it was between me and another guy and I headed up to Laramie to the refinery's offices for the deciding interview. But it was a difficult drive, where's AmoShah when I needed him? I thought then. Why wasn't this heavenly connection thing of some use! If this heavenly vision is authentic, then why do I get stuck with so much interference? I was getting messed with by demons the whole trip, and what the heck! Well, I didn't get the job, my emotions were being hammered while at the Interview, and it was one time I didn't do well. Normally, I got compliments from the interviewer as I interviewed very well. Not that day, I was getting jerked around much too hard. Later that day, I was walking about downtown close by my apartment in Fort Collins and hearing excuses from AmoShah and thought. This smells like fish in Denmark and went after him and cast that deceiving spirit out. It was a demon all along, ever since that night with Joe's junk and the "spirit-baby" scene, when this [clone?] must have been introduced. Why hadn't the Heavenlies told me, what the...? On another tack, I was meeting with the gal that recommended the Ana Captivity book to me. She and her prayer partners were doing deliverance "Ana style." I still couldn't figure this out, if this was genuine and of the Lord or not? She tells me her recipients are reporting real progress, "and this was a good and very useful approach." I was wondering just what the real deal was? That week I met with the worship leader at church, George.

And he and I decided it might be useful to consider Ana style deliverance for him. George had a screwed up set of early years and was still working through their affects. People that suffer childhood issues and are not Christians are in extra deep trouble. How can they get to the roots, the damages from the abuse? Christians have a terrible time when working through the results of childhood issues with the Holy Spirit's help! How can the unsaved be expected to survive? It could have been a lot worse for me in this battle; I thought then. So, I met with George and we got right to it, and things were about as they had been at the last meeting, the previous one I had with Betty's group. George noted some intriguing happenings that seemed truly genuine, and we departed. A few days later I got a call from George, and he reported that on the following day he had a deliverance session scheduled with Cindy. At that meeting, Cindy found wicked spirits from Ana's (Voice of the Light) ministry, an Ana spirit, spirits of deception and delusion, and I was bemused and quite intrigued. Could this whole Ana thing have been a deception? Later that day, I stopped by to see Bro Mel; we talked for a while, and he confronted me with the news from George. Further stating that the Lord was rebuking me and got quite upset. But I thought, cool, now I know at long last, and I told Bro Mel I repented and I meant it, and I'm done with all that Ana stuff. I owe Bro Mel for many hours of doing his ministry to help me. I recognize that and remain grateful for those efforts.

The lesson from Ana's captivities ministry was this. Any demonic contamination, any at all, was entirely too much contamination and has to go! Period!

My personal sanctification clearly remained an uncompleted project; there were a ways to go yet. Especially in getting clear of the demonic, the fight was still on. So, it was back to the apartment and to combat. I was still doing self-deliverance "deliverance in detail" style, and got right after the top dog; I reasoned they'd been discovered and had to answer up, and they did. I found a prince demon who was a spirit of deception, and under its headship a small group of power spirits. Spirits of delusion, confusion and deceit, and kicked the lot out!

A Spiritual Warfare Ensemble

Fantastic, NO MORE VOICES! Yes, Lord.

It was long awaited silence. Blessed silence; just my thoughts were in operation and no more chatter, thoughts that were entirely mine, wonderful! I don't believe that Ana meant any harm, no sir. I think that she got an answer to prayer that was intended to come to her aid in her particular family situation, back then. And it got turned into a ministry. We do make mistakes; we do that kind of stuff us Christian folk. But we do have a God that will call that to our attention and at the right time to deal with it. I'll continue to trust that is what happened here.

I have noticed on her website that the Voice of the Light Ministry hasn't had a deliverance conference in quite a long while, years now. I wish she'd taken her Regions of Captivity book off Amazon and their website, but hasn't.

"Looking Back, an Overview"

≈≈≈

Now, I think that blown job interview was a deliberate exposure point. What would have happened had I continued on with "AmoShah" despite all the red flags? The demons would've joyfully begun operating with heightened permissions that's what, resulting in a deeper deception. Agreement would've sucked! As the "earthly" AmoShah was a deception, resistance to that deception, repentance from its influence and the casting out of the thing put the brakes on to anything more from that "Ana" quarter.

"Thoughts to Take Away"

≈≈≈

Allow delusion, allow that, and demons will be quick
to
strengthen the lie.

Chapter-Thirteen

- Don Dickerman Ministries -

So good, no more voices and this is beautiful, cool. But am I entirely free? Is this the end of the haunting? Well, not so much. There were still difficulties with sleep and I noticed other things, but it was hard to figure them out. Rob called and congratulated me on the elimination of the voices, and asked if I could do some house sitting for them as they vacationed. There'd been some burglaries in the area he said. So it was off to Austin arriving at the end of May and I beat the heat, even better as Austin can get scorching. While I was there I fed the cats, cleaned up their minor messes and chased them with Rob's toy helicopter - just a bit. I was looking after things in general and helping with the lawn and plants and walking about, walking all throughout the neighborhood. I wanted to exercise the ticker by taking good brisk walks and they were doing OK those walks, but just OK. Not like I'd wished. Maybe it had something to do with being sixty-six?

A few weeks passed and I was headed back to the Fort. But, after arriving at the airport in Denver things weren't right, I wallowed in dizziness and confusion? I found myself walking over the same ground, sigh, and repeatedly getting lost. Eventually, I found a place to sit and relax and worked on sorting these things out and putting a plan together. This strategy worked and got me through the airport. Then it was onto the shuttle, back to the transfer point in Fort Collins eager to collect my car. OK, there was the car; I thought, and realized that I was gasping like a fish out of water, I was just flat out of breath, which was odd. Driving the car was weird too; it felt somehow disassociated and unfocused. But I made it back to my digs and up the single flight of stairs, and paused at the first floor landing. Thinking this is all wrong! I was utterly exhausted, again. Next day, I could barely walk to the supermarket a block and a half away. Bad news; I'll have to start another recovery, again, like after previous heart attacks but now, without the heart attack.

A couple of weeks later I made it to an appointment with my cardio guy. He was a young, sharp, cardio surgeon with uncommonly skilled hands. A chance find from my local Heart Center Group. And amazingly, he seemed to realize that I tended to find my own solutions as money was extremely tight, and I did better if left to my own devices. He checked the results from some blood work and said, "you didn't have a heart attack," and to, "keep on keeping on" and got up to leave. I got alarmed and angry and told him that. Hey Doctor, quite frankly, I was fed up with all these temporary patches. Challenging him to do a full angioplasty and get a complete picture of my heart's actual condition. He thought a moment and replied, with the shortness of breath I experienced; it's justified. So, OK, on with the show and the procedure was scheduled. It's a week later now, and I'm on the table in the heart center for my angioplasty. I can't see much from the x-rays displayed on the massive, multi-monitor display as they viewed the dye transitioning through my heart. I did note that my surgeon didn't seem too happy with the results. We met a bit later to look things over, and he said, "You're going to need five stents in the near future."

And I said, "no way, that's clearly not acceptable" and he agreed with me and asked my thoughts. Earlier in the hospital, in pre-op. I'd queried the nurses, asking, "Who's the best surgeon." Who was their best "Mr. Hands," the top choice of chest guys? I said it's time for a full cardio bypass; he agreed and agreed with my choice of surgeons. The "Mr. Good Hands" man. I got an appointment and the doctor looked over the pictures from the angioplasty and was unsure if I would benefit from CABG, which is the heart bypass grafting surgery and said. "You can control this with statins." I protested and said statins are garbage and flat poisonous to me, purely trash! He looked sheepish and related that he'd tried them himself, "And they liked to have killed him." Then he excused himself to get a consult with some other surgeons. After a short time, he came back and said it's OK, let's do it. "I understand about the statins and agree." Then we booked a surgical appointment about a month off. The funny part is, in the month to go, I cut back on the walk-a-bouts and eased off regular exercise and felt great. It was better than I'd felt for a long time.

If I didn't know better, I'd think I didn't need this procedure done at all. (Could there have been any demonic influence there too?)

It's funny; people think the demons are so single faceted. Don't they always lie? Nope. Aren't they all liars and cannot speak the truth, nope. It's a matter of what suits their purposes, if they needed to speak the truth to find a way to hurt you then the truth is spoken. Please understand this, their mission is to deface the image of God in mankind, hoping to make God a liar. They cannot attack God Himself, so they sneakily go after the sole creation directly created in the image of God, us. And in this particular, if they could produce a sensation of well-being in hopes that you'd overlook your operation. You're liable to feel pretty good, and they're quite adept at what they do. But, they can be held accountable. Remember this. They will lie to us, but if you require them to speak truthfully or lie to Jehovah God, they'd genuinely prefer not to lie at all, they will be punished for that. But give them a juicy target like injecting a bit of confusion or doubt into a deliverance session, and they may well take one for the home team and attempt to lie to Jehovah God. We have the guidance of true God, Holy Spirit, and can discern when a lie is attempted, and can then rephrase the question and get the correct answer and confirm that. A manner of interrogation you'll see in the Jenkins deliverance script. Keep it simple that works the best confound them with simplicity and authority.

I was feeling quite energized, back then, and came to this conclusion, that the lack of oxygen in the blood supply from a limping ticker had produced a subtle high. No wonder high blood pressure is called a silent killer. That is, if this is one of the ways a lack of oxygen can act, and I think it must be. And what about the demons? One's who may be dodging my deliverance efforts. And what if I can't hear them? Are they are still hidden away and still trying to move against me? So I got with Bro Mel and Cindy and asked them to get aggressive and get after any family curses or heart related spirits. And Bro Mel took this very seriously and gave me a wide-ranging deliverance and curse breaking session.

A Spiritual Warfare Ensemble

Thanks again, Bro Mel, what you do, you can do exceptionally well!

God Bless!

The staff counselors at the hospital tried to prepare me for what was in store, but they failed to present an accurate picture. This CABG procedure works well for younger and more robust patients; they seemed to take it in stride, but that wasn't me. On the Internet, the stories varied, but the one that struck me as relevant said it had to be experienced to be understood, and that sounded ominous. So I stocked up on frozen burritos and frozen vegetables, and figured I would probably need a two-week supply. Then I got the place extremely well cleaned and as ready as I could. I thought an ordeal was coming my way and tried to set things up so I could deal with it; that is without too much outside help; I couldn't afford that. I was still not sleeping well, but by now. That seemed to be life for me, and I was somewhat resigned to it. I made all the necessary arrangements, got my will updated and was physically and spiritually as prepared as I could be. That was despite any remaining demonic interference; I still thought there was some kind of oppressing presence hidden away within. So, OK, I was off to get fileted.

The anesthesia was stunning, one minute I was on a gurney, and then I was transferred to a surgical table - execution style. My arms were stretched out like at an execution, and my back was arched, and hey that hurt, and its lights out! Next, I awoke in a recovery room, cold as ice. The bed was vibrating, and there were tubes in me and guess what, this was miserable. This was greater physical misery than I'd experienced before. It was all dull-throbbing's, annoying vibrations and intense-shaking from the cold; it clearly sucketh. The nursing staff kept coming around and annoying, and that's a part of it. And it's no sleep and can't you fix the vibration? The bed is vibrating! Next, it's off to a lower-intensity recovery room, and it was still cold, freezing cold. The temperature controls were located right where I couldn't reach them, and the air-conditioning was blowing directly on me, and it's again, sad.

132

Sorry for the negativity but that's what happened, and it's as usual, the expedient, rather than the well-thought-out in this life. And in this medical field, when considering the weighty charges attached, it should be much better thought out! Darn right! I did manage to get up and start using the John and moving about, and pleaded with the nurses, "why can't you stop this blasted vibration?" Really! And finally, a nurse heard me. She checked and said my heart was out of rhythm and hooked up a bag of meds, and that stopped that. There were breathing exercises to go through to restart and fill the lungs and this was not good. I was seriously determined to get out of there. The human body does not like being "dead" for an hour or so. The effects are so broad and bone tiring that it's quite impossible to anticipate. This is an excellent condition to avoid and boo on all processed foods, the roots of this condition. Twice, I am awoken at night, bathed in sweat, with the sheets soaked with sweat, doing spiritual warfare in my well drugged sleep. The hospital population of demons was after me. I got myself organized and at every chance; I was up and walked as far as allowed. When I was permitted to continue, I practiced getting up stairs, wandering about, and exercising so I could get back to my apartment. No sir, you can't go home I'm told; you must go to a nursing home for a week. Bet me! No, I won't be charged for money that I don't have, I won't let this impoverish me. I'll go home in a cab, and I'll sign whatever forms you want me to, but let me out of here. They had their revenge. I had to walk an awfully long time to get meds I didn't want or need any longer, and then I was outside in stifling summer heat waiting for a cab, great. I arrived at the top of the stairs shaking with fatigue, and ticked.

Notice a pattern here? I did my best to get ready for all this and made my plans after some careful research. Things were clear in my mind, as best as I could anticipate, and it got screwed up and confused; I wondered how? It couldn't have anything to do with the opposition? Could it? Or is it the demonically tinged system in this thoroughly fallen world, and then the heavenlies chiming in, the flesh too, or is it all of the above? All the time!

My rickety old body didn't like having its heart stopped and worked on for an hour. It seemed the rest of my body decided since the heart had stopped that it must be dead too, and it shut down as well. The recovery was slow, and a visiting nurse noted my frustration and the fact that I didn't like being beaten by all this. But I was; I was beaten, I was defeated. As soon as I pushed myself just a tad bit too far I had to pay a price, a steep price in starting the recovery all over again. One afternoon I was washing dishes, and I reached up to put a plate away one time too many. I spent the next four hours sitting on my couch, cell phone in hand. Trying to figure out when I had no choice and needed to call for an ambulance. I waited it out until I finally stopped shaking and gasping. There just wasn't a way to make myself heal quicker. For the first time in my life, I was subject to the full consequences of all the hurt I'd done to myself and what I'd suffered from otherworldly, spiritual powers. So, it was slow and steady, and yes, I'll go wash the bike and do the dishes and the laundry, yes slowly. It was largely, try to do a wee bit at a time and try not to lift very much as eight pounds was the max. And Lord, why does it take so long to learn patience?

It was terrific that I no longer heard the demons, but sometimes I'd catch them messing up and getting too obvious, like when they'd press my frustration buttons too hard and often. I'd go after them and evict the suckers, and then that too came to an end. I was at the point where I would go to war and find I had no one to fight against. But, I reasoned that the hospital had to have made a contribution to my plight, so, once again. It was time to go looking for what to fight with, and what weapons to wield. I still had full liberty remaining to obtain, and an uncompromising dedicated enemy to find and expel. There were happenings at Church too. Brian Melvin had been going to a Lakota Indian Reservation; he had relatives there. He was preaching and practicing deliverance, him and George our worship leader. So I got busy and bought a capable printer to print out the pamphlet's you'll see in the "Bonus Section." There must be well over a hundred copies put to use in the Indian reservations, and still more at Church and that's cool.

I continued to buy books on deliverance for the church (you'll see them listed in the pamphlets and the End Notes,) and created a lending library. But that was more of a donating library as so few got returned. But that was okay, as long as they were helping people – this was part of my contribution to the church. When I was working it was easy just to tithe on paydays, but now I was too poor, and those were good books; they fitted in well, quite useful. At home, in my "senior retirement" apartment, I'd started looking through the Amazom.com recommendations, and it became a daily exercise. And when the Holy Spirit fingered a book I'd buy it and read it. Well, with one, I didn't understand why He'd chosen it. It was from a nationally known "big wheel" in spiritual warfare at a very well-known church in Redding, California. This book didn't ring true. It seemed that this author had little personal experience of attaining freedom from the demonic. And what about personal sanctification? It seemed he hadn't heard of it. And, (this was the part that burned me up) when he failed to deliver a person, it was their fault, exclusively. For quite a while, I failed to understand why the Holy Spirit selected this book for me.

I'm thinking now, that it was so I could learn this. That distinction in an area of ministry doesn't necessarily mean deep understanding, just prominence. Maybe, the fuller understanding will come later, and then I made a fantastic find, a book that looked intriguing. When checking the reviews it seemed to speak about reality with a solid ring of authority. It was by Don Dickerman, a preacher who had a long-term and productive prison ministry. In it, Don told of how his prison ministry got extended by the Holy Spirit into the area of deliverance, and of his practice of deliverance. I bought this book and read it thoroughly, re-reading it, analyzing it and trying out his examples and finding new areas to explore, areas that yielded tiny demon populations. Aha, terrific, a new weapon! And then, I enthusiastically read a second book by Don on the same subject. And discovered there was truth there too, and got some encouraging results. These books were *"When Pigs Move In"* and *"Keep the Pigs Out."* So, I happily called south and recommended these books to my friends in Austin. Then when they'd read them. I started bugging them to go up to Fort Worth, up to Don's offices and get delivered. I called a few times weekly.

My messages went something like this: "This is the Fort Collins bugging service calling. Have you filled out the questionnaire on the Dickerman website yet? Thank you and good day." Eventually, they got their questionnaires submitted and made an appointment. Rob told me that he had not ever, not even once, heard a demon speak. He's an engineer and just too analytical; he thought. So up he went to Fort Worth to get delivered of his strongholds and was quite impressed. And he did, indeed, hear the things as they snitched on one another and exposed the structure he'd been fighting, blind. His wife had a similar experience and is a fan of the ministry now. Rob stated that he didn't think the deliverer had any special discernment. But that the methodology used was just incredibly powerful and that anyone could learn to use this approach and without too much effort. It was my turn; I filled out the questionnaire and sent an additional three pages, as their questions did not go to many of the places that I'd been. And I wanted help with the whole shebang, help with anything I couldn't deal with on my own. And so, I thought a lot more detailed history was called for.

I received an appointment card and release form to sign and mailed it in. Then, setup flights from Denver, making arrangements for staying with Rob and Lisa, as the cats may need chased by the toy helicopter, just a bit - you never knew? As my time for the appointment drew near, I got terribly sick – boo. So, off to Vitamin Cottage, a good health food store to get some liquid vitamins and minerals, which for once did not stop my flu-like symptoms. But the stuff did make me well enough for the flight – life can be difficult. My appointment at Don's office arrived and I met with the staff and we made small talk. At one point, the conversation drifted to my side. I told the story of how I hadn't the funds for this trip. Not until there was a night of intense windstorms, including a blast that blew the cover off my Sporty and turned it into a sail. That sail blew the bike against a neighbor's car. Rats, I'd said then, quite disconcerted. I picked the thing up and checked out the damage, sighing away. The next day I e-mailed photos to the insurance company, and they were willing to pay for the cost of the parts on the bike, leaving the repairs to me.

My neighbor got her car repaired in a local shop, and I got the money for the trip, cool. They heard lots of stories like this one. So, Reginald (Reginald is a pseudonym for one of the deliverance team members), and I went to a private room. They'd read the questionnaire and my accompanying letter and understood them and used them to produce another questionnaire. And we got right to it. They asked a series of questions to determine whether or not I was qualified and prepared for deliverance. Quite different from Bro Mel. And, once that was addressed, we went to questions about specific topics checking for moral and personal issues. Issues that I and the Holy Spirit had already dealt with. Then, moving on to find the top dog, the prince demon in charge. Aha, what's your name spirit? And we were off. Reginald found a structure hidden away, first a prince demon and then a whole army of the things. On interrogating this "reference spirit," it turned out the army came from Jane, surprise, surprise! Reginald needed to know more about Jane, and after my relating some of the goings on with her. Reginald composed something like a small script for gathering the demons together for convenience in casting them out.

And then ordering them to clean up their messes, which I cannot remember. When you're undergoing deliverance, you think you'll remember what is going on, but not actually; you're too busy. He went after the army, cleared it out and then was on to the rest of the structure he'd found, and commanded healing from all the damage they'd been doing. And that began right then, and we were through. Reginald explained that I'd done a great deal of work, and he was right about that! Back in my borrowed Van, headed south, back down to Austin. My chest was tingling, healing from where the demons had been attacking it; it stayed like that for a long while. Also, since the surgery, my chest had been numb from the incision outwards. But later, I discovered that there was a small area on the left side that was still numb, but the rest felt about normal. I thought that was curious, and I wondered what else had been healed. During the last few weeks before the deliverance, I'd been feeling badly enough that I hadn't written a "symptom sheet." A "symptom sheet" is a listing of your thoughts on just what your felt symptoms were, they'd requested that. This was a full accounting of feelings whose source, whose roots I was unsure of.

Distinct things say like a sense of anxiety or features of my person or character which I wanted to explore. Things I wanted help with to discern what was not of the Holy Spirit or me, and get after them! That was the primary reason things had gone so fast. Without that input, there remained overlooked areas with a demon content left intact, lingering within.

I think it often works like this; there can be many prince demons commanding a person's strongholds. And some of the demons may not even be aware of the other's presence. It's such a dirty, chaotic mess within. Pastor Jenkins's Deliverance Script and the Dickerman Ministries, function by the interrogation of "a reference spirit," and binding the demons to an explicit behavior. They do this by using a biblically structured, comprehensive, Holy Spirit powered process that leads to the demons expulsion. They are compelled to leave because the truthfulness of their answers to the deliverer's interrogations and their commands too, are continuously verified as accurate and obeyed, or not. Their obedience is always checked, they just can't slip away. So accurate and complete information is needed beforehand, or you wouldn't know where to pursue the spirits or understand if you'd gotten them all. Necessary information would include a listing of a person's symptoms and often multiple sessions would be a logical approach. You want to remove any structures, any strongholds or loose demons, and any symptoms demonic content – entirely, completely.

When talking with Reginald after the session, I asked for additional information. He rummaged around in a file cabinet and gave me a small selection of DVD's and said "that this was about the best around." I knew the deliverance I'd received was incomplete. The remaining things were harassing me and some nights, sleep was difficult. The flight home was fine, and no problems showed up at Denver's airport - unlike the last trip, the one before my surgery. The following day I was feeling fine, and at the apartment I loaded up one of my new DVD's, a "Marty Quinn Deliverance, a Teaching Tool" and ran it. I played this disk again and again. The recording's content was the most exciting thing I'd seen yet in deliverance. This was a really stirring example of why I'd missed attaining a full deliverance; it simply went places, I knew nothing of!

The original recording happened about twenty years ago and was a deliverance done by a Pastor Bruce Jenkins. It appeared to me that Pastor Jenkins was working with a prepared script, and I wanted to learn it. Unfortunately, the video's audio was limited in spots, and I wasn't able to grasp all of its bits and pieces, so I called Texas and got his phone number. Next day, I called Pastor Jenkins and asked for five copies of the book he'd written, *"Set at Liberty – A Warrior's Manual."* Pastor Jenkins book was written more for a counselor than a layman, and a lot of it went past me. Especially in the second half. Had I been a trained counselor, I'm sure I'd have gotten it all. But, towards the middle of the book he had included the deliverance commands and methods he'd used in his forty-year ministry. Aha, it must have been quite similar to what he used on the video, cool, an extremely shiny new weapon; thanks, Lord! I typed the books entries into my laptop, turning it into a script, and lightly re-ordering it. Sorting it all out, working to get the hang of it, leaving as much of it in the original as I could. Decision time Paul, what's it going to be, now or later I thought? You're kidding me, right? I jumped on it! Quickly jotting down my thoughts onto a symptoms sheet. Writing into it any felt symptoms one line after another and dropping down.

I'd list whatever I'd thought of as a symptom, and another thought - another symptom, then let it sit for a bit, letting it cool off some. When of a mind to, I'd sit down, consult the symptom sheet in creation, listing anything else I thought suspicious. Any symptoms that "might" disclose any demonic activity; anything physical, mental, spiritual or emotional that I thought suspicious. I came back to that sheet repeatedly, continuing on with this for maybe, five days. Meanwhile, I had re-read the script and book it came from until I said enough, I'd learned the subject well enough and went to war. I read the opening prayer from the script that sets up the deliverance session, aloud, and bound the wicked spirits to obedience. I was blocking off their favorite tactics of delaying and shuffling around and about, and then sneakily hiding out; no nonsense allowed. This is strictly business. Holy business. First off, to get a (reference) demon's name and use him to discover the top dogs over my symptoms. I was a bit stunned as there were smaller numbers of demons associated with and helping to aggravate all my symptoms, cool; I'd nailed it. That's the input from the true Holy Spirit; this was super - thank you Lord.

A Spiritual Warfare Ensemble

After dealing with the symptoms, and getting the correct number of demons listed for each, I began going through the script, dealing with the rest of the categories. Calling out and sorting out the demons. I recorded all this on a print out of the script and kept it all tidy. Call them out, sort them out, throw them all out, all done in a well-organized and extremely difficult to evade manner. The key to this was pretty straightforward, know the enemy and allow for no variance; their obedience was required. The commands I was using were issued in the power of "the Name of the Lord Jesus Christ." And were always checked and confirmed as obeyed. Or, by continually checking the demon's response as accurate by querying; "Will this stand as truth before Jehovah God?" This script worked remarkably well. When things started to get a bit confused, or it didn't seem as though I wasn't getting them all, the Holy Spirit helped me out by revelation, and they did not escape. That Sunday, I was talking to Cindy after Church and showed her my new symptom sheets with the names of the vanquished prince demons over my symptoms, along with their count. Also, I told her about the different spiritual locations in the soul, the mind, will, memories and emotions. Then the flesh and adjacent areas that the script called out those demons from.

She looked interested, other dimensions? What other dimensions she asked; I've since learned that there are three dimensions we deal with in spiritual warfare, and they are our flesh, this fallen world, and evil supernaturalism. This script, when used with a symptom sheet is thorough enough to use as a benchmark: a reliable standard to judge by. A tool to employ over and over again for use in maintaining one's freedom, cool, excellent. The next week, I started another symptom sheet, got prepared over the following four or five days and went to war. I continued in the same way as earlier. I found about half my symptoms had demons connected to them, and things went smoothly and well. The following morning I felt fantastic. I hopped down the stairs deciding on where to do my morning walk-about, feeling like I was on steel springs, just like when I rode bicycles for long distances. How neat! My body had responded to this new level of freedom with a great walk. I felt like this was one of the nicest of all spring days, what a spiffy treat, and this continued on for a few more days. That Sunday, I showed Cindy my new sheet and told her my new testimony, and she left with a grin.

The following week, I prepared a new sheet, a short one. In just a few days I was done, and went to war and found NOTHING! Nothing! Wow, what a relief. Finally! Later that day while taking a break in a sandwich shop, by the local University just enjoying my lunch. I realized something: for the first time in my whole life, I liked myself! What a sensation; all my life, I had been living under the impression that I wasn't good enough. Too skinny, to this, to that; it was demonic. And now that they're gone, I like me, for the first time ever. Thanks, Lord, really.

Now, today, this is the best part, and it's this,
It's that I'm now on the path To True Sanctification.

≈≈≈

The word sanctify means to be set apart for God's use. If you are sanctified, God can use all of you; you are set apart from evil and for good. A person who seeks holiness by withdrawing from all evil, but does not seek any positive service is not biblically sanctified. Jesus said, "For their sakes, I sanctify myself. I set myself apart" - John 17:19 and that's not just from evil, but for good. Sanctification happens through the word of God, which is truth, so it involves those who receive the word of God as truth. And I do.

≈≈≈

Coming up is the "Jenkins Script." I'm back in missions and continuing on, and things back home are better now. The Church is getting cleaned out and under less attack, for the most part. This freedom is now mine to keep, the enemy shows up a bit from the outside, now and then. Especially after a deliverance session where I've used the Jenkins's script setting someone free. But it's small potatoes now and not much of a problem, not again.

As I close this section and think back on this testimony of mine. If there's one thing it's proven conclusively, it's this, that we all need the Body of Christ. In my case I needed it for my very survival. Without the efforts of those working to help me, it could have been much worse, and it could have been lethal. But, my deliverance. That could have been a whole lot better too, and thus this book. My case was quite extreme, my poor brother Walter. Should you need to use this writing as a sort of guide please do, and don't feel bashful about setting up help from Bro Mel or Cindy or Don Dickerman's ministry, just do it. Pastor Jenkins says he's swamped. Then engage and destroy those spiritual enemies, and as you do so, you'll discover the depth of the oppression against you, and have these excellent resources to work from, and you'll do fine,

God is good, and enough is enough.

Next up,
The Pastor Jenkins's Deliverance Script.

Set at Liberty,
A Warrior's Manual

By Pastor Bruce Jenkins, which contains this
text, and as he said, it is here for your
use in full or in part.

First Published 2001
≈≈≈
Used with permission from Pastor Bruce Jenkins

A Spiritual Warfare Ensemble

*T*his script was originally written as an example of Pastors Jenkins ministry efforts and from the standpoint of ministering to a new deliverance candidate. It does require that a person be lucid IE: able to hear from the enemy, and just report what's being said by the demons. When working with someone new to deliverance, you may want to start with their symptom sheet in order to find that first spirit to interrogate. And, after finding that initial demon power, work your way up the hierarchy of the demons from there. As it's presently set-up, you're going after the highest-ranking evil spirit overall, the reference demon. Then, onto any other spirits unveiled by the symptom sheet and any strongholds and individual wicked spirits until free.

It further assumes that the candidate received an introductory letter. That letter would have asked them to list things in their lives that are out of order, not of them, and not of the Holy Spirit either, and that they are suspicious of or didn't want. A symptom sheet. As it's presently edited. It's set up so you can just use the Find/Change or Replace feature of your Word Processor, and change the name Alex to whatever name you wish. Replace the name "Alex" as it appears in the text, and make changes as necessary to get a nice clean copy. The commands for evicting the demons, are typically indented and are mostly in bold, and the comments and explanations are in Italics. Take notes, and work at keeping all of this in good order, as you would not want to overlook a category or a symptom.

Then, script in hand, go directly for the most powerful spirits, the prince demons. Get their count and demote them when you choose, I'd suggest right away. Lastly, please read through this text getting familiar with it before you get started.

Lord Bless.

B egin with commanding prayer aloud. In the name of the Lord Jesus Christ, I now bind every spirit anyway associated with Alex (last name), whether in him, attached to him, or any way connected with his life. I now call you demons under the authority of the living and resurrected Lord Jesus Christ, the One who defeated your master. You are commanded that you will not harm him nor leave him and go to someone else. I command that you will not split, divide, multiply, fragment or clone, nor use any form of demonic trickery or deception. If you have already split, divided, multiplied, fragmented or cloned, you are commanded to rejoin as one kingdom. There will be no passing on of duties, nor calling on others to replace you. All traffic will be one way, and that will be out and into the abyss, the pit of Hell.

I forbid the use of revolving doors, and any entry by other demon powers. I command that you dissolve all intentions. All demonic works will cease, damages and disorders will be repaired and restored, exactly as Jehovah God intended. Now, whether in deep hiding or sleeping, using shelves or dark corners. In the sub-conscious, coming and going or floating in free circulation, you are now under the authority of the Lord Jesus Christ and you will be obedient. All hiding places are destroyed. I remove all crowns and robes of authority. You are commanded that you cannot communicate with other demons at this time; you are not to plan, plot or scheme and devise in any way to retain any kingdoms. All kingdoms will be completely and utterly demolished. Satan you are bound from sending, or lending any outside assistance or interference.

To demons present, you are commanded to retrieve every seed that you have planted. You are commanded to uproot everything planted, nothing will be left behind, you're to leave no residue, and every doorway will be closed and locked. The command in the name of the Lord Jesus Christ is that, when directed to, that you go immediately and directly into the abyss, the pit of Hell and never return. I now command that you demon powers, lineup in order of rank. I separate the highest-ranking demon from the other demon powers and command that you will stand alone, gaining no strength from other evil spirits. "This is the command of the Lord Jesus Christ, and you will obey it!" I speak to you demon powers, and I unstop your senses and give you speech.

This initial prayer used with permission from Don Dickerman Ministries

Now Command:
"In the name of the Lord Jesus Christ, I command the highest ranking demon power associated with Alex, (surname) that you come to attention, and you come to the front. What is your name spirit?" Get the things name. *(If the spirits resist, delays or ignores you, pray to our Lord Jesus Christ for the help of His heavenly angels to compel the demon to answer your questions. Give it a moment. Then you get a name.) For an example, I will use the name "Fear" for this deliverance's reference demon. This is the one that will stay with you; it's there for you to interrogate until it's the very last one to be evicted. This demon knows every demon power associated with that person, and can see every one of them, and who knows them by name. You can now use the symptom sheet to command (in the name of the Lord Jesus Christ,) that this demon reveal the names of any other demons associated with this person's symptoms, or any structures or strongholds, and wicked spirits present. Then with the symptoms sheet in hand, go after all of them in order.*

Using the name obtained from the highest ranking spirit, say: "I command to know if there is a demon power associated with the symptom (as an example) of fear of man." *You're working to build a listing of all of the demons. Make sure to get a name and be sure to record that name, and please don't try to rely on memory alone.*

If the demon replies "yes" and that is confirmed as fact before Jehovah God – You know that there are demons present associated with that particular symptom. *It could be any symptom you picked from your symptoms list. And remember, you are using this method by the authority of the Holy Spirit granted to you to do, just this! Then, get the name of the prince demon over that symptom.* At that juncture, get an accurate count of the demon powers present and confirm for that symptom.

Regardless of whether you get a "yes," or a "no," you will ALWAYS cross-check every answer, with, "Will that stand as truth before Jehovah God?" Demons will lie to you, but experience has proven that a demon will not willingly lie to Jehovah God. Keep your questions short and pointed, a demon may be tempted to lie to Jehovah God if it thinks you have given it enough room to hurt you! And it may be necessary to remind your deliverance candidate. Who is obviously lucid? That if they may need to, in the very beginning go with their gut feelings, and that's just fine.

Next Command:

In the name of the Lord Jesus Christ, I command you demon Fear (or the reference demon) that you are bound at attention, and you cannot move." *Demons are generally named after the symptoms with which they are associated. But, their names can be anything. For example; let's say you command the spirit to,* tell you if there are any demon powers associated with the symptom of Fear? *And you get a "no," ask, "Will that stand as truth before Jehovah God?" If the demon replies "yes" then there are no demons associated with the person for that particular symptom.*

If the demon answers "no," you will know that the demon was initially lying – he had to change his answer to line up with the truth. A "no" reply to a cross-check means the answer is opposite to the first answer he gave. In this way, as you go through the symptom sheet, you will arrive at a correct listing of the demon powers associated with the person's symptoms. *Call them out, sort them out, and cast them all out. Again, always check all replies with the query: "Will that stand as truth before Jehovah God." Cut them no slack, they won't allow you any! When you have finished the listings from the symptom sheet move onward, advance to the strongholds.*

Now Command:

"In the name of the Lord Jesus Christ. I command you demon Fear, are there any demon powers associated with the real Alex. The one redeemed by the Blood of the Lamb which are impersonating Alex?" *(Demon's will impersonate the true Holy Spirit, tongues, the Lord Himself, and the Individual themselves as a method of hindering and blocking the Holy Spirits work. And yes the prayers of the saints too.) Cross-examine any answer to verify "yes" or "no."*

You need to repeat this command for any nicknames the person has used in the past, or is presently using. *You want to leave no place for any demon powers to hide. Don't be surprised if you get a "yes" to these commands – counterfeit demons, like counterfeit tongues are very common. Counterfeit demons can be whom a person has conversed with, thinking they are speaking to the real person. I typically command to know how long this counterfeit demon has been associated with the real person. And, you may get an answer of, "since birth." In the spiritual world, birth is the moment of conception – and that WILL stand as truth before Jehovah God. Tell that to an abortionist! In the real world, the spiritual world, a child is a person at the moment of conception. Add any demons found to your list.*

Now Command:

"In the name of the Lord Jesus Christ. I command you demon Fear, (or the reference demon) are there any demon powers associated with the real Alex in the subconscious that have not been reported?" If you get a confirmed "yes," ask how many. For example, if the number was five – ask "in the name of the Lord Jesus Christ. Will it stand as truth before Jehovah God, that five is the sum total of all demon powers unreported in the subconscious?" *Don't let them hedge; continue questioning them until you get the correct confirmed and accurate count.*

Then, In The Name of the Lord Jesus Christ:

"I command you demon Fear, (or the reference demon) are there any unreported demon powers associated with Alex, in free circulation?" "In the name of the Lord Jesus Christ. I command you demon Fear, are there any demon powers associated with Alex. One's that are hiding, who are in deep hiding, sleeping, or using some form of trickery that we have not been told about?"

"I command you demon Fear (or the reference demon) are there any demon powers associated with Alex in any other dimensions that we have not been told about?" *If the confirmed answer is "yes" to any of these commands, and the number is four or less, I always ask for their names. You can do so for any number, especially if you have fewer overall demons to deal with. You can get rid of demons, either by knowing their names or by knowing the exact number you are dealing with.*

There is one other area that you need to check. Query this: "In the name of Lord Jesus Christ, I command to know, are there any demon powers associated with Alex that are shared with other people, and that have gone to those other people to avoid exposure?" *"After you have verified all the facts, and the answer was "yes" command."* "In the name of the Lord Jesus Christ, I command those demon powers that attempted to avoid detection that you gather up your works, the residue of your works, and all your associated demons. I command no passing on of your duties; you will come immediately and entirely to Alex and be bound in him, you cannot move." "I command you demon Fear, (or the reference demon) in the name of the Lord Jesus Christ, are there any other demon powers associated with Alex?" *You now have accounted for the strongholds and structures, to continue.*

You Now Command:
"In the name of the Lord Jesus Christ. I command, do you de-mon Fear, do you or any demon power associated with Alex have any ground or consent that has the approval of Jehovah God?" *If any demon has consent that will stand as truth before Jehovah God, you must command the demons to reveal what the person has done to give that consent, record that. As you received a "yes" answer, re-spond with.* "In the name of the Lord Jesus Christ. I command that all demon powers associated with Alex that you are bound at attention, and you cannot move – I cause a spiritual division between you and the real Alex." *Now you can talk to the real person and get him to confess (if he is indeed willing to repent as sin) the consent he had given. Which you recorded and to reclaim, in the name of the Lord Jesus Christ all the ground and consent he had given to the enemy.*

Now call demon Fear (or the reference demon) to attention. And command to know if he or any demon power associated with the real person has any consent remaining, and will that stand as truth before Jehovah God. If the person covered all consent, you will get a "no" – and then they have no further consent.

It Is At This Time That I Command:
"In the name of the Lord Jesus Christ. I command (name EVERY+ALL demon powers [excepting] demon Fear, all those that you have recorded as being associated with the person). That if you have any multiplications, divisions, or shared demons you will unite with them into one demon by your respective names, immediately and totally now with no passing on of duties." Now ask the reference demon that you have been dealing with, "Has that command been obeyed?"

The demon may say "no" and if that answer will stand as truth before Jehovah God, understand there are only two ways that a de-mon can disobey the command of the Lord Jesus Christ. (1) Either God gives them that consent, and by now you will have verified that issue as resolved by repentance. Or, (2) the other way by which they can disobey is if the person wants to keep the demons.

If the demons acknowledge the person wants to keep them, ask, "Will that stand as truth before Jehovah God?" *If you get a "yes", you need to bind the demons at attention again, cause a spiritual division, and ask the person why he wants to keep the demons. It is neces-sary that the person confess as sin, the desire to keep even one de-mon, and to speak aloud to the demons, "I do not want to keep any of you demon powers." That issue is now resolved. But, if the demon confesses that it will NOT stand as truth before Jehovah God, then the demon used a delaying tactic! With this knowledge, you can now compel the demons to obedience.*

It Is Now That You Command:
"In the name of the Lord Jesus Christ. I command that all bits and pieces, scars and workings wrought by any demon power in the life of Alex, his mind or body, are removed from him and welded to you demon powers. You will leave no residue, no remainder, and withdrawal demons behind. All that you demons have wrought in Alex is now welded to you, demon Fear." *By covering the withdrawal demons, you may spare someone addicted to smoking, drinking, or drugs the trauma of having to go through withdrawal. Also, if a physical affliction was confessed by the demons to be demonic in source, that area should be very apparent by the presence of healing. I have seen instant healing multitudes of times.*

It Is At This Point That You Command:
"In the name of the Lord Jesus Christ, demon Fear (or the reference demon). I command to know if you, or any demon power associated with Alex are hereditary in nature. And have been associated with him or his genealogy, for two generations or more?" *If you get a "yes" that will stand as truth, command,* "In the name of the Lord Jesus Christ. I command that you tell me the name of the most senior ancestral demon." *When you have confirmed the name of the most senior ancestral demon (assuming that there was a confirmed "yes" to the previous command.)* Command him to come to attention, and to come to the front. Command to know how many generations he has been associated with his genealogy. *After confirming as truth the number of generations,* ask if it will stand as truth that he is the most senior ancestral demon.

Then command, "In the name of the Lord Jesus Christ, I command to know if you, or any demon power associated with Alex are functioning under a curse upon their generations." *Please understand that curses are real. God recognizes the right of a curse to stand until it is broken. People are putting curses on people today. If you get a confirmed "yes" ask if there is more than one curse. When you have confirmed the number of curses upon their generations, then, command to know the nature of the curse(s). It can be anything – murder, rape, and sexual perversion – ad-infinitum. After confirming the nature of the curse(s) command.*

152

"In the name of the Lord Jesus Christ. I speak to the curse(s) of (name the nature of the curse(s) you have recorded,), and I destroy them. I put them to naught; it is as if they had never been." Now command, "In the name of the Lord Jesus Christ, I command that all ancestral association of all ancestral demons with his genealogy are herewith destroyed." *Being sure to record the count of those ancestral demon spirits. Add the demons found to your list.*

At This Point, As The Person Is Lucid:
"I will command the demon to tell me the name of his lord," *and when he has confessed that Satan is his lord. I command him "to look around and see if he can see his lord anywhere." When he says, he cannot see him anywhere. I tell him, that's the kind of lord that you have – he has deserted you – Alex's Lord never leaves him or forsakes him, but you demons have been forsaken. If a person is lucid, the fact that the demon has acknowledged Satan to be his lord will be important. The Christian person would never confess Satan as his lord, but those words will have come out of his mouth. He would never admit to such a thing, but, someone did. It must have been a demon. This knowledge will make it difficult if not impossible for the enemy to convince the deliverance candidate, that nothing happened, that there was nothing to their deliverance!*

You Are Now Ready to Cast-out the Demons, at this point you Command:
"In the name of the Lord Jesus Christ. I command you demon Fear (or the reference demon,) that you are bound at attention, you cannot move. Nor can you hinder any demon power in their obedience to the command of the Lord Jesus Christ." *Then I speak to every demon power, and I name every demon – other than demon Fear, the reference demon.*

"In the name of the Lord Jesus Christ. I command that you demons in your entirety, gather up your works, the residue of your works, and all of your associated demons, I command no passing on of duties. All demonic works will cease; damages and disorders will be repaired and restored exactly as Jehovah God intends. I sever you from Alex, and I command that you come out and go completely and utterly, and directly into the pit of Hell. In the name of the Lord Jesus Christ, you go there NOW!"

Then I pray, "Father, I claim the promise of your Word where it says that when two agree as touching any one thing, it SHALL be done. (Matthew 18:19). Heavenly Father: I ask you to fill every area vacated by the enemy, with the presence and power of Your Holy Spirit.

Now Call Demon Fear: (or the reference demon) **to attention and Command:**

"In the name of the Lord Jesus Christ. Demon Fear, I command to know if demons (here again, call every demon on your list, [except] for demon Fear) have, in their entirety, obeyed the command of the Lord Jesus Christ, and gone into the pit of Hell?" *Whatever the answer cross check it. It will have to be a "yes" – unless demon Fear (or the reference demon) is trying to pull something on you. By now it has been well established that no demon has a right to disobey the command of the Lord Jesus Christ. With the "yes", you know that every demon power that you named is gone INTO the pit of Hell. Now you should have only one demon left, demon Fear.*

Command, "Demon Fear, will it stand as truth before Jehovah God that you are the only demon left in association with Alex." *Unless there was some demon that has been successful in hiding. You will get a "yes" Whatever the answer. Do what you must do to ensure complete freedom and victory for the person to whom you are ministering. With a "yes", you know that all demon powers except demon Fear are now in the pit of Hell.*

Now Command:

"In The Name of the Lord Jesus Christ, demon Fear:" "I command that, if there are any demonic kingdoms here, other than that kingdom associated with you, that those hidden kingdoms are herewith dissolved. And all demons associated with those hidden domains are welded to you demon Fear. With their works the residue of their works, and all of their associated demons, I command no passing on of duties." *Now, demon Fear, were there any hidden kingdoms dissolved and any demons united to you?" If you get a confirmed "no" then you are ready to deal with demon Fear. If you get a confirmed "yes" then command. "How many kingdoms were dissolved, and demons united to you?" Get the confirmed number of domains and the demons from the hidden kingdoms, command…*

"In the name of the Lord Jesus Christ, demon Fear, how many demon powers, from the (number of) hidden kingdoms, were welded to you?" After getting the confirmed number of demons from the hidden realms. Command, "In the name of the Lord Jesus Christ, demon

Fear, you are bound at attention, and you cannot move. I speak to the (number of) demons that came from the hidden kingdoms. I unweld you from the welding, herewith; I welded you to demon Fear. And I detach you from him, and I command you to gather up your works, the residue of your works and all of your associated demons. I command no passing on of your duties, and you come out of Alex and go immediately, and entirely and directly, into the pit of Hell. In the name of the Lord Jesus Christ, you go there, NOW!" *Now confirm with demon Fear that those demon powers have obeyed the command of the Lord Jesus Christ and gone into the pit of Hell. At this point, you know that there is only one demon left in association with the person" and you should have a confirmed "yes" then you will command:*

"In the name of the Lord Jesus Christ. I command you demon Fear (or the reference demon) that you gather up your works, the residue of your works, and all of your associated demons. I command no passing on of your duties, and I sever you from Alex and command you to come out and go immediately, and entirely, and directly into the pit of Hell. By command of the Lord Jesus Christ, you go there NOW!"

Now pray, *"Father. Thank you for complete victory for Alex. I ask you to fill him so full of the Holy Spirit that there would be no room for the operations of the enemy or the working of the flesh. Now tell the person to look you straight in the eye and to try not to blink. Say to them, "I want a yes or no answer, I don't want any other explanations, and I only want a "yes" or "no." "In the name of the Lord Jesus Christ. I command to know, are there any demon powers associated with you in any way?" If you get a confirmed "no," from the person you know that demon Fear is in the pit of Hell and the person feels and understands that freedom. At this time, it's a good idea to check for the presence of a hidden spirit with the role of silence. As if it's present, when checking for spirits hiding at the end of the deliverance. The candidate will have another batch of spirits sheltering under it, and the person wouldn't have heard anything from it earlier, as its very function was silence. Finally with a confirmed "No" from the person assume the person has 100% victory from demonic spirits. And - if not, follow up later on, starting with a fresh symptom sheet. Continue on until you hit on empty, entirely and completely empty!*

Deliverance Script Notes...

Lastly, if during the deliverance process you find strong resistance you may find it beneficial to demote all of the demon princes. Command, In the name of the Lord Jesus Christ,

*"**I command you demon(s)** (numbers of demons – or individual demons) that you are no longer a demon prince, but I shrink you down in size to that of an insignificant imp. I strip you of all power and authority and place you subject to my commands, in the Name of the Lord Jesus Christ. It is done!"*

Most often I call the demon princes at the opening of the deliverance and just demote them then to get them out of the way, why bother with nonsense from them is my thought. The reason you are calling for the most dominant demons at the onset is they are in authority over the others, you are following the "chain of command."

This is largely the text contained in the book "Set at Liberty" by Pastor Bruce Jenkins. It corresponds well with the "Casting out Demons" Teaching Tools video produced by Don Dickerman ministries, http://www.dondickerman.net/, or, You Tube Video's - "The Deliverance of Marty Quinn." Lastly, I typed this into Word.docx so you can edit or make the best use of this for your own deliverance efforts.

Should you want this script emailed to you, send me an email, and it will be in the reply. Specify .doc -or- .docx, moehrinp@gmail.com

Please print this as an 8-1/2" X 11" sized page for use in deliverance, as both a script and note paper.

156

– End Notes –

≈≈≈

H aving put this book together, as it is. I've been concerned for those folks who cannot hear the demons when they are called forward. In looking for an answer to this dilemma, particularly regarding self-deliverance. I'm recommending another book "The Handbook for Spiritual Warfare" by Dr. Ed Murphy. This weighty work answers any honest questions that can be brought forward against the practice of deliverance, and exhaustively uses scripture to answer any objections. It provides a history and illustrates the appropriate role of spiritual warfare in Jesus's day, as well as today. Most importantly, it's structured as a counseling and deliverance model that has been tested and been proven effective. In reading it, I realized that if I was unable to hear the things I'd want to go to this source of help and put it to use.

"Requirements for Deliverance"

≈≈≈

– The following is an excerpt from that book –

Be assured of salvation through personal faith in the Lord Jesus Christ.

Humble yourself before God.

Be totally open and honest with Him.

Confess and renounce the sin of your family line.

Confess and renounce your own sins.

Choose to forgive everyone who has hurt, rejected, or offended you. Especially those who have injured you the most deeply (as an act of faith and obedience; your emotions have nothing to do with the matter.) Asking God to forgive, redeem, and cleanse those who have hurt you. Desire (by faith) their salvation and spiritual well-being.

Commit the totality of your life to the absolute Lordship of the Lord Jesus Christ. Speak out against Satan and his demons declaring

157

they no longer have any place in your life. Their sin grounds have been removed. They must now leave your life and never return.

Recommended Websites

Don Dickerman's website:
    http://www.dondickerman.net/home.html

Bruce Jenkins's website:
    http://www.gospelpioneers.com/details.html

Amazon.com:
    http://www.amazon.com/
        (Addresses tested and working May 2015)

≈≈≈

Books sold on Amazon.com & Recommended Here

- Soul Ties and Legal Ground - by Jessica Jones
- Iniquity - by Ana Mendez Ferrell
- Prayers that Rout Demons - by John Eckhardt
- When Pigs Move In - by Don Dickerman
- Keep The Pigs Out - by Don Dickerman
- The Handbook for Spiritual Warfare – by Dr. Ed Murphy

(Titles tested and working May 2015)

You Tube Video's

"The Deliverance of Marty Quinn"
By Pastor Bruce Jenkins
https://www.youtube.com/watch?v=hZs1_XLpkG4

"A land Unknown Hell's Dominion"
By Brian Melvin
https://www.youtube.com/watch?v=h2X5uAB692A

(Video's tested and working May 2015)

For all of those, unsure of their Personal Salvation

Please consider this, "that God's delight is received upon surrender, not awarded upon conquest. The first step to joy is a plea for help, an acknowledgment of moral destitution, and an admission of inward paucity. Those who taste God's presence have declared spiritual bankruptcy and are aware of their spiritual crisis. Their pockets are empty. Their options are gone. They have long since stopped demanding justice; they are pleading for mercy."

(Max Lucado, God's Promises for You: Scripture Selections from Max Lucado (Kindle Locations 375-378). Thomas Nelson. Kindle Edition).

≈≈≈

This need not be all that complicated, just earnest. As an example; from Reverend Billy Graham's "Final Sermon" on His 95th Birthday. Dear Lord Jesus, I know that I am a sinner, and I ask for Your forgiveness. I believe You died for my sins and rose from the dead. I turn from my sins and invite You to come into my heart and life. I want to trust and follow You as my Lord and Savior. In Your Name.
Amen.

≈≈≈

For all those using this Jenkins's Script as offered, in full or in Part

Once you have a reference-demon used to being confronted with the demand. "Will this stand as truth before Jehovah God?" And have used the script and symptom sheets to achieve a through cleansing thus far. Consider this, that this demon also can identify the need for the cleansing of one's iniquities. To recognize and report open and unlocked doors, and to be aware of a person's idols and spirit ties. And the books recommended in these End Notes, they will help supply the particulars for dealing with these topics.

An Excellent Letter

How I Learned to Pray for the Lost

Here is a remarkable testimony which should be a real help to many. Since the nature of the testimony is personal, the writer requested that her name be withheld. "This is the result of my search for the right way of praying for the unsaved. I have found it to produce amazing results in a very short time. After more than 20 years of fruitless praying, it seemed that there was no possible chance for my loved ones ever to return to the faith. But after only a few weeks of the type of praying that I have outlined here, I have seen them studying the Bible by the hour and attending every church service possible. Their whole attitude toward Christianity has changed, and all resistance seems to be gone. I have taken my place of authority in Christ and am using it against the Enemy. I have not looked at myself to see if I am fit or not; I have just taken my place and have prayed that the Holy Spirit may do His convicting work. If each and every member of the body of Christ would do this, what a change would be made in this world." Believers everywhere are burdened for unsaved or backsliding loved ones. However, many are praying in the spirit of fear and worry instead of in faith. This has caused me to seek for definite light on how to pray. Feeling the need of praying the right prayer, and also the need for a definite promise or word from God on which to base my faith when praying for the unsaved. Praise God—He never fails to give such needed help. Perhaps because the salvation of some seemed to me to be an impossibility, the first verse of Scripture that was given to me was Mark 10:27, "With God all things are possible." The next Scripture verse had occupied my attention for some time, but it took on a new meaning. "For the weapons of our warfare are not carnal, but mighty through God to the pulling down of strongholds; casting down imaginations (speculations) and every high thing that exalteth itself against the knowledge of God and bring into captivity every thought to the obedience of Christ" (2 Cor. 10:4, 5). This shows the mighty power of our spiritual weapons. We must pray that all of this will be accomplished in the ones for whom we are concerned; that is, that the works of the Enemy will be torn down. Finally, I was given a solid foundation for my prayers—the basis of redemption. In reality, Christ's redemption purchased all mankind, so that we may say that each one is actually God's purchased possession, although he is still held by the Enemy. We must, through the prayer of faith, claim and take for God in the name of the Lord Jesus that which is rightfully His. This can be done only on the basis of redemption. This is not meant to imply that, because all persons have been purchased by God through redemption, they are automatically saved. They must believe and accept the gospel for themselves; our intercession enables them to do this. To pray in the name of the Lord Jesus is to ask for, or to claim, the things which the blood of Christ has secured. Therefore, each individual for whom prayer is made should be claimed by name as God's purchased possession, in the name of the Lord Jesus and on the basis of His shed blood. We should claim the tearing down of all the works of Satan, such as false doctrine, unbelief, atheistic teaching and hatred, which the Enemy may have built up in their thinking. We must pray that their very thoughts will be brought into captivity to the obedience of Christ. With the authority of the name of the Lord Jesus, we must claim their deliverance from the power and persuasion of the Evil One and from the love of the world and the lust of the flesh. We should also pray that their conscience may be convicted, that God may bring them to the point of repentance and that they may listen and believe as they hear or read the Word of God. Our prayer must be that God's will and purposes may be accomplished in and through them. Intercession must be persistent—not to persuade God, for our redemption is by God, but because of the Enemy. Our prayer and resistance are against the Enemy—the awful owner and ruler of darkness. It is our duty before God to fight for the souls for whom Christ died. Just as some must preach to them the good news of redemption, others must fight the powers of darkness on their behalf through prayer. Satan yields only what and when he must, and he renews his attacks in subtle ways. Therefore, prayer must be definite and persistent, even long after definite results are seen. We must pray for the new Christian even after he begins to be established in the faith. We will find that as we pray, the Holy Spirit will give new directions. At one time, I was interceding for a soul and began to feel that my prayers were largely ineffective. When the Holy Spirit inspired me to begin presenting that person to God in the name of the Lord Jesus. As I obeyed this leading, praying, "I present so-and-so to God in the name of the Lord Jesus," I felt that my prayers were gradually becoming more effective. It seemed that I was drawing that person from deep within the very camp of the Enemy. Then I was able to proceed as usual claiming every detail of that life for God, using the power of the blood against the Enemy. This is true warfare in the spiritual realm. Thank God that our spiritual weapons are mighty and that our authority in Christ is far, above all, the authority of the rulers, powers and forces of darkness, so that the Enemy must yield. It takes faith and patience and persistence.

––––––

Reprint from "Back to the Bible" broadcast.

Bonus-Section

≈≈≈

Self-Deliverance Pamphlets
to Follow

Self-Deliverance 101:

A "Quick Start" handbook,
which will help you to defend yourself
- Today -

Edited for clarity, April 2014

This is a pamphlet I wrote in the midst of combat, you may find some of this information quite useful. But let me be entirely clear, this manner of deliverance did not bring me the freedom I sought, not as the "Pastor Jenkins Deliverance Script" did. What helped me the most was using multiple, concurrent, Holy-Spirit filled deliverance approaches! Along with the Bible, books about the Bible and Sanctification, the Body of Christ well involved, that's what did it.

Please take a moment to read this before getting Started.

≈≈≈

This pamphlet assumes there is a full demonic infestation in place, and you need help right now! This will not be the case for many of you. But, there is a wealth of information here. Information that may well contain just what you need. Read through this pamphlet and begin prayerfully exploring to find what you could use, and utilize it. Determination and a willingness to try to help yourself and others can make all the difference between being a victim or an over-comer! Your spiritual enemies hate and despise you. You will find clear descriptions of what you may be facing in these pages. And the knowledge that can aid you into adjusting your attitude and methods of defense; awaits you. Trust in Jesus and his Word as your foundation, and explore this information to see what you can use, and use it repeatedly!

Self-Deliverance 101

About the Author

I 'm Paul Moehring, of Fort Collins, Colorado. And I wrote this pamphlet in the midst of continual combat with demonic spirits so that I could remember what worked and how. In brief, I come from a demonized family. They didn't realize it, and I didn't either for most of my life, and I'm now 65 years old. At age 18, my older brother Walter was admitted to a psychiatric hospital in New York City. He spent one-third of his life in such ghastly places as a full-blown schizophrenic. My family thought he suffered from a mental disease, which he did, but mildly. What drove him utterly mad and finally killed him were demons. A few years ago when Walter died, strange things started happening in my life. At first, it seemed that my spiritual life had suddenly been jumpstarted, especially when praying in the spirit and interpreting tongues as I did then. But there was something suspicious; I heard beautiful things, sometimes too fantastic? I arranged a trip hoping to learn what might be going on and set out some fleeces. When I returned from the trip, things were not as had been promised (by the supposed, holy spirit.) And so I challenged that spirit that I was hearing, when I interpreted tongues, and all Hell broke out, literally! "What, you dare to call us liars!" suddenly boomed into my mind, unbidden! I was immediately hit by nausea, blinding confusion, oppression and depression. My back was in knots from tension and tears were streaming down my face from the pain.

Voices I couldn't control, and couldn't stop, were screaming at me in volumes that would mask a stereo turned very high. Full-blown spiritual warfare, intended to destroy me had begun. It was organized by scads of demon spirits that had transferred to me from him after my brother Walters's death! I endured almost three years of constant conflict until I eventually evicted legion after legion of demons and defeated the warfare sent against me from the pit of Hell! That kingdom which seemed to use all of its available resources, continually, against me! I was not alone in this. There was the pastor from my church and a handful of deliverers, Godly ladies that had suffered from and defeated demons in their own lives, and the church's help found in deliverance ministries in the US. The church for me, then. Was largely the "Body of Christ" as I discovered it over the Internet, and in books, whether recommended by friends or prompted by the true Holy Spirit. This pamphlet is an accurate reflection of the contest that was my everyday experience. That battle was documented by my emails to friends, serving to prompt memories when I found it necessary to look back on those days. Looking back so that the misery I endured, might help others and be an example of what may be defeated and how. That is if they apply the lessons of the Bible and are willing to accept and try what others in differing ministries make available!

I want to thank Brother Mel, pastor of All Nations Church and Deliverance Center in Fort Collins, Cindy Richards and her team members and the following authors for the books listed. Soul Ties and Legal Ground - by *Jessica Jones*, Iniquity - by *Ana Mendez Ferrell*, Prayers That rout Demons - by *John Eckhardt*, When Pigs Move In - *Don Dickerman.*

Finally, my thanks to the folks at All Nations Church!

Methods for Self-Deliverance:
There are more steps here than may be necessary, depending on your needs, or, the variety of spirits you want to be cast out! Some people are able to hear the spirits, some not so much. Yet all these approaches are useful to help ensure that demonic spirits cannot find a way to remain inside you; they destroy the spirit's claimed "rights to remain." Self-deliverance requires that you are a Christian believer. If you are a believer attempting the deliverance for a nonbeliever go for it, use these steps, but, firstly, bring them to the Lord! These lines of attack cover the bases well. Be sure not to skip any until you have found your stride with these interlopers!

Assume the spirit we are going to cast out is named "Taskas." Consider (Taskas) lives with other spirits in a cluster that functions in the area of unbelief. **(Note: Please read through and grasp the essentials before beginning self-deliverance.)** *Start off by commanding all spirits in a given area, 'unbelief' in this case, to come forth...* "In Jesus' name I command all spirits that act in the area of unbelief to come forth! Come forth in Jesus's name! Now! Come forth spirits!" Assume Taskas is answering up, he's a spokesman for a bunch of spirits, most likely (what? with a bit of surliness.) "Spirit what is your name! I command you, tell me your name!" You may have to pry its name out by getting its assignments first. Eventually, it answers [my name is Taskas] and you decide to kick it out right away. (If you don't hear the spirits at all, that's fine, look for symptoms. Try to find the root cause and attack there.)

Self-Deliverance 101

Here's a proven method for your use.

Assume there is a strongman present:
"Strongman I bind you and despoil your house!" Continue by binding the particular spirit. "Taskas I bind you!"

Cancel assignments:
"Taskas, I cancel your functions and tasks and take authority over you and command you to still all operations against me during your expulsion."

Isolate the spirit:
"Taskas, I separate you out from all principalities and powers, wicked spirits in the heavenlies and any spirits in me. You may not be enabled, encouraged, strengthened or given anywhere to hide! Taskas, I sever all connections to principalities and powers, wicked spirits in the heavenlies and to me!"

Remove all attachments:
"Spirit, I command you to entirely remove all attachments to me!" Sever links. "I sever all ties or bonds from unholy spirits to me!"

Break curses:
"I break all curses against me, no matter their origin, including forebears, blood, or familiar, or territorial, or accusing! In Jesus`s name."

Renounce:
"Taskas, I renounce you! You are a trespasser and an interloper and an unwanted spirit!"

Fall out of agreement:
"Taskas, I fall out of agreement with you. I pray to my Lord and savior Jesus Christ asking Him to cleanse me and forgive me for all acts of agreement I have ever made with any unclean spirit in Jesus's name" Thank you, Lord. Lastly, I apply the Blood of the Lamb to cleanse me!

Casting out:
"Taskas go, I cast you out. Go spirit, go, completely, entirely, all the way out leaving nothing, and not-one of your underlings or associates behind, not a wisp! In Jesus' name go, loose from me spirit, loose in Jesus's name! Go spirit go, all the way out, go, in Jesus's name be gone!" Continue in this manner until all manifestations, - burping, expelling gas etc., stops. And eventually a feeling of relief occurs, then

do it some more! Keep at it until you are satisfied that the spirit is entirely gone. It's a completely personal response that varies from person to person, and maybe you'll have no reaction at all; look at the results over the coming days. Lastly, check for the spirits' presence by attempting to call it forth as you did in the beginning. **(Note: If an evil spirit begins to speak out-of-turn or manifests trying to intimidate or confuse. Command it to "stop speaking," - "be still," - "go down," - "peace be still," etc. Just get right after it!)** This whole process may take just a few minutes or many minutes, depending on the level of infestation and number of spirits you decide to evict at one time. At first, you may need to go after the spirits that torment you the most. Later, when you gain more freedom, then you can go after them all, whatever kind of spirit has an effect on your life! Self-deliverance is an essential step for an infected believer to embrace. This technique will help a person to reach freedom, along with an effective Christian deliverance team; wherever you can find one. *And you've got to find one you can't do all of this alone!* All concerned parties need to stay in touch and work together. That's the ideal way to obtain freedom from demonic spirits. Also, there is a compelling responsibility for the believer to work for their own deliverance. We are told by Scripture to work out our "salvation with fear and trembling." And that's our personal sanctification process, and we want this deliverance process to be as prompt as we can make it.

Additional Help:
We started off assuming that you found a spirit named Taskas. And that there are more spirits in that cluster; you can call them forth and make a list. Tie all the spirits functioning together - figuratively, and literally, by making the motion of tying them together while telling them what you are doing in Jesus's name. Do the same when you are separating them out, (make the motions of cleaving between areas with your hands.) Why? Because these spirits observe every movement you make, and every word you utter! Utilize that. The spirits recognize when the person targeted has learned their position in Christ and is determined to clear them out! Yes, they can fight back. Expect them to attempt to dissuade you from coming after them by any means they have. Your best response is to make yourself as much of a "demon unfriendly environment" as you can. Making yourself into a bad house for them! Play Christian music often, attend church at every opportunity, and seek out people who have some experience with this and are willing to help you. And most powerful of all, remember to come against them in the "opposite spirit", always confound them! Lastly, yes, all this is a bit like bad science-fiction and

will remain a bit unreal, a bit unworldly. Judge the process by its fruit. Make a good friend, a confidant. One who can give you a reality check when the spirits "mess with you." Wicked spirits are capable of the most dastardly actions, they have no mercy, none! It's a lot like dealing with a really crooked lawyer. Be careful of your language and attitudes; you just want to get free! If they try to make you get mean with them, don't fall into that trap. Your anger would allow them to ratchet up their harassment!

Explanation of the steps applied earlier:
These steps were tested and retested in pastor-to-person deliverance sessions and self-deliverance. They have been retested by others, and reviewed by participants and found to be valid and useful. They are an amalgam of biblical example, biblical exhortations and revelations of the Holy Spirit in individuals acting in deliverance ministry.

Command the power spirit in a given area to come forth:
Require the spirit to identify itself by its name.

Bind the strongman:
You bind the strongman as an opener because Satan's kingdom is a well-organized machine. It's dedicated to mankind's destruction and the individual's downfall. When people are afflicted with demons, there often is a structure involved. It's based on status, power, and bragging rights! You and I are the disputed territory until the arrival of the Holy Spirit in authority and truth. Then it's a contested evacuation, with as much damage as they can do until they're discovered and expelled. Within a person is a demon hierarchy, large or small depending on the amount of infestation. When someone has a presence of spirits in such a quantity that drives a person to seek help, we can safely assume the demons have an organizer in place. That's the strongman. Bind that sucker! Tie it up! Keep it from interfering with your candidates for expulsion! "I bind you strongman, in Jesus's name!" Just like that.

Bind the specific Spirit:
You bind the spirit for expulsion so it is restricted in its activities, and doesn't have full freedom to infect others or to avoid its removal.

A Spiritual Warfare Ensemble

Isolate the specific spirit:
Isolate the spirit so it cannot successfully duck its expulsion and cannot be enabled by other spirits. Continue on to help prepare the spirit to be cast out by removing all its ability to claim a right to remain in you!

Remove all attachments:
You want to remove the means the spirit actually uses, to attach to you. This will positively affect your longevity on the earth, your health and energy.

Sever links and bonds to yourself:
When you sever the links and bonds, you limit the ability of clusters to organize their resistance, and you help sever the spirits claimed rights against you

Break curses:
Breaking curses is essential! No one can fully know their antecedents and what has been transmitted by their family bloodline. People are born all the time with powerful curses - bondages that have been passed on to them by a distant relative. Being born into a Christian household affords wonderful protections into a child's life. Many of us didn't have that advantage and have been "messed with" by spirits since before our births! Boo! Time to get free!

Renounce, fall out of agreement:
During our days, various spirits have been ambushing, influencing and misdirecting our emotions and working to get us to unknowingly agree with them and act out their intentions. This is always to our detriment and is the same to those around us. It is a continual battle requiring the "opposite spirit" to keep them from having, "a place" set aside, in our lives for them. Sometimes the spirits are so subtle that the attacks are undetectable, confusing, (Where did that come from?) or just too fast; the moment had passed, and the damage was done. Or, we just get accustomed to their activities! Falling out of agreement and praying for the remittance of the sins done under their influence and cunning will dramatically undercut their claims to belong in us!

Cast out:
All right, time to get free! Go spirit, go! This is the fruit of the expulsion process. The spirits' claims are undercut, you flat don't want

them, and furthermore, reject and eject them! You're using the authority that Jesus gave us when He returned from the grave, offering this power to mankind for their freedom. Yes, the Holy Spirit will rule in authority and truth! Feel free to modify this guide as you discover what works best with you. Mark it up, there's plenty of room, but please keep all the elements in play here, as it covers a lot of territory.

Possible demon organizations:
Check for these spirits in an individual over the course of their deliverance. It is a basic structure, often used by demons and can be found in many individuals.

MASTER SPIRIT - A high-status spirit that leads the entire attack against an individual. It can have any function, any role.

STRONGMAN - A key spirit that directs clusters of spirits or an attack against an individual. These spirits will shift around as you clear out their memberships!

BEACON OR ANTENNA SPIRIT - A spirit who advertises to other spirits your availability and prospects as a suitable long-lasting abode for them.

GATEKEEPER - A spirit who opens and shuts inner gates to admit or allow spirits to enter, leave, or transit within you. This spirit acts as a boss or organizer. It can reassign spirits to continue an infestation or resist your deliverance.

POWER DEMON - A spirit that is typically more powerful and has many helpers. These insidious spirits really want to remain to do more damage. It is always great to throw any of these spirits out!

WICKED SPIRIT - A general purpose spirit, found in any function.

DEATH SPIRIT - As stated, often vicious when they are strong. They can mount attacks to shorten your life through heart attack, emotional breakdown, or give you a slow and painful death.

Please note: When all these spirits are short on power they tend to lay back. It may be if they are unable to do anything really nasty, they become resigned to being kicked out. There are very many spirits that can infest an individual. You should check for the presence of any of these spirits as clearing out the leadership is a fine way to defend yourself. All of this lends a powerful hand in your complete deliverance from evil spirits. To the glory of God in the grace of the Lamb - get free!

Proofs, further steps, and other stuff:
As you've gotten this far, you may be wondering just where all this information came from? Well, it's from the Bible, experience, and revelation. It's funny, many churches dispute deliverance, often from a denominational position. Other churches avoid this area entirely (they just overlook it,) so folks needing help often are pretty much on their own. This is not the way Jesus intends, it's just the way it is in our current church environment. But, with or without effective churches, Jesus gave us an instruction book to study so that we may become confident in His truth, and obey it.

Mark 16: 17-18	Luke 10:19-20	Matthew 10:1
Luke 4: 18-19	Acts 10:38	Matthew 8:16
Matthew 4: 23	Luke 13: 10-16	

There! Now you have scriptural ammunition to strengthen you and give you greater understanding. Be sure to *read these scriptures in context*, as this will clear away a lot of denominational gripes. What you practice is what counts! Jesus delivered men, women, and children from the deprivations of demonic spirits. He questioned the spirits, and repeatedly, verbally, commanded them to leave a person. He even chided his disciples when they couldn't cast out a demon, and cast it out himself. In plain, clear language the Bible shows that demons are real, present, and remain within a person. That is, until a believer, who understands God's Word and lives a godly life, stands up and evicts them. Yes, that means even you. Health issues may well dissolve as the spirits are thinned out, or they may just heal naturally as a person gains their freedom. The Word states it, demonstrates it - deliverance to all in need. Jesus has given each individual the right to come against evil spirits in His name. Deliverance is one of the duties of the church at large. It is not going to come from a nice "feel-good" sermon over the TV. It's up to us to use what has been provided for us at such a terrible cost. Thank you, Lord!

Discussion of demonic behavior:
Demons are real spirit beings. Some are vicious, and some are personable and more relaxed, and others are sneaky. Most are cranky and all are just interested in getting their way. All the better to destroy you! They are individual spiritual creatures and; some even get embarrassed when caught in their tasks. They have some respect for those who stand up to them and cast them out, even as they work against them. Demons fear believers in Christ who know them well. They despise mankind, and plan together for the destruction of anyone who willingly yields to them. They will torture them at every opportunity while causing all manner of mayhem! When demons feel threatened they will: run for help, curse, scream, and, yes, joke occasionally, get ticked off and become resentful and stirred up when confronted and cast out. They hate it when people come against them in the *opposite spirit*, that is, to oppose them by doing the *opposite of their urging*, this is so very effective! They will often speak deceptively, in half-truths to shade perspective or twist knowledge to their advantage.

Some spirits of deception can imitate the effects and presence of the Holy Spirit with great cunning, yet eventually they give themselves away as there is no true godly power possible for them. Some people hear them clearly. Some see them as in a silhouette. Many folks hear them and report what they hear in order to assist the deliverance team. Remember, many does not mean all; this is a very individualized process! As stated earlier, it's much like coming up against a really crooked lawyer. The evil spirits must respect truth, and they must go when commanded, or, they will have to pay a price later. When the spirit lies to the deliverer, it is lying to the Holy Spirit. It can be likened to ignoring speeding laws; speeding will catch up with you eventually. So, you tie a number of spirits together and go about casting them out, and then a few days later, you find one of them someplace else. So you address it. Wicked spirit, how did you defy the power of the Holy Spirit? [I hid] You hid, why? [I was scared!] Maybe on an occasion you missed a step. The remedy is to revisit areas where you've been casting out, such as where we started with "unbelief." Call that area up and check for spirits. Also, as you proceed through the ranks of spirits, others will come forward out of hiding, replacing spirits lost with a similar function as theirs; some were dormant! Perseverance counts, again, it's a lot like peeling an onion! Demons may quickly abandon their houses when an individual recognizes their position and authority in Christ. A demon has to give way as a person applies scripture and just goes after them. Peel that onion! This handbook works to cover the bases so demons have no legal or moral grounds to resist eviction. They will get accustomed to being under your attacks as you go about clearing them out. And this process will get easier and quicker. It's essential to pray for healing after they are gone. It also helps to ask Jesus for healing when they appear to have left, as that will often clear out the last wisps of them! Also, as they go, claim for yourself all the territory that they have left vacant and give it to Jesus!

Helpful steps to utilize:
Let's say you've found a powerful spirit that defies you, and will not yield. If you've determined its name, applied these methods and it continues to mock you, command it like this, "Spirit, I drain your strength! Like electricity going to ground, your strength is drained!" A spirit will, usually, complain; they hate this. Next, send them to Jesus. They will shortly be on their faces before the Lord of the universe; that thought makes them unhappy! Sometimes you just cannot get them to budge. They have built up an armoring of other spirits that they will throw to you as sacrifices. Then they'll run and hide like in a game. Sometimes, you can verbally sprinkle the "Blood of the lamb" on their hiding places, forcing them to answer up, and truly identifying themselves. Often, you just need to keep coming at them, and coming and coming. Persistence will rule the day! Keep after them, and remove their armor, bit by bit. Don't quit.

Sometimes the power spirits are such bullies that the other spirits will stand aside and allow you to get at them! They fight, and snitch on each other, and enjoy seeing enemies getting thrown out. They will also lay traps, trying to catch you in some sin. And they will bait you, hoping to get you to try to hurt them so they can raise the level of harassment in response. Just keep after them! Respect yourself. You are a child of God. Demons are creations too and deserve a modicum of respect because of that. But no more than that! So utilize scripture, the folks that are helping with your deliverance, and this guide, and stay on them!

Some rules demons respect:
They want to be named - they want to be identified by their preferred name, the name by which they can be cast out. Spelling and pronunciation are big with them. Status is a great part of their motivation. If they will not give you their name, get their assignments. Cancel their assignments in Jesus's name, and then go back to getting their name. If the demons have responded to your calling them forth, and

you already have their function and their assignments. You've got a good enough handle on them already. They should give up their names soon enough! Then follow the steps listed before to scoot them out; with or without their name, they must go!

Demons crave respect:
Demons sleep, get tired and confused and make mistakes! They hate it when you learn their secrets and inform others about them. They must respect the Holy Spirit and obey Him. There are limits to their harassment. The Holy Spirit sets those limits so we are not over-whelmed by demons, despite their numbers. Never, ever, yield to any demon's orders or directions. Do not have conversations with them. To do so will give them a deeper level of rights to you! Really, really avoid that! Always oppose them! One spirit will be the spokesman when a group is interrogated. The other spirits in that cluster or function are subject to the spokesman. But when cast out, they do not leave all at once but in order. So, when there are a number of them they can be compressed into one demon to aid in their removal. They are spiritual creatures and exit like gas. Some people burp them out, some expel phlegm (no, it's not vomit), some fart, some scream, many shake and some are silent showing no reaction at all.

Later the delivered person describes the positive changes in their lives. The thinking, the speaking and intelligent part of the demon ex-its at the last. And yes, they can be cast out rapidly, and by the dou-ble handfuls! People can be infested with large numbers of spirits. They tend to work together, in tandem or with just a few active in one area, with many dormant, who are waiting an opportunity to act or to be called forward by the upper-level spirits. They tend to replace each other in their specialties, their functions, and are crippled work-ing by themselves. Yet we need to get all of them thrown out, no, not just the top ones. The more demons threw out in a session, the bet-ter, and the more frequent the session, (daily is recommended!), all the better. As it takes a while for them to bicker and feud their way into a new organization after taking their losses! Also, as you tackle the spirits and remove those in the upper levels, eventually they will find themselves without leadership! At that point, some harassment will drop off and the probability of them restocking themselves will be lower.

Opportunities!
Sounds funny, right? In deliverance? An opportunity for what? Well, how about knocking back the opposition!

177

A Spiritual Warfare Ensemble

Here are some examples:

- An evil spirit manifests, you get the feeling that a wet blanket has come over you. It makes your skin crawl. Yuck! Well, try this: "Spirit that is manifesting, what is your name? Come forth spirit. What is your name?" Get after it! Or there's a thought pattern that continuously replays in your mind. Evil spirits are doing this. The function is called "a racing mind," say: "Spirit that is manifesting as a 'racing mind,' what is your name? Come forth spirit. What is your name?" Get them.

- Depression is an evil spirit as well. "Spirit that is manifesting as 'depression,' what is your name? Come forth spirit. What is your name?" Go after it!

When dealing with emotions, you may not be able to find the spirit behind the emotion, at first. With persistence, you will, as you peel that onion. Begin to notice when something is not of God and not of you. That is likely from a demon. You are winning your deliverance - they just gave you an opportunity. Work through the listings above. Go for it, in Jesus's name!

Self-Deliverance 201:

Moving on then, getting-them-out
by the double Handfuls

Edited for clarity, April 2014

There are:
Three principle categories of spirits' susceptible to these rapid deliverance methods. We'll recognize them as symptoms, functions and locations. You can best use these techniques after the deliverance team or deliverers, you are, hopefully working with, will have helped you get to a greater level of freedom. Then, while continuing to work with you, you reach your own (more matured) level of authority, and these techniques will really come into play. Make that into high gear!

Know that:
We will also be working to remove three levels of demonic trespass: 1) Active (Those that are up front and coming against you that possess underlings and associates). 2) Inactive spirits (These are aware but not directly involved, with subordinates and associates). 3) Dormant spirits (Spirits awaiting an opportunity to get involved, by sin or by being called into play by higher level spirits). That is the enemy!

Our object:
Of course, is to throw out spirits so fast and so often that they remain unable to take the offensive as they would otherwise! As for the spirits themselves, I think they just need to be treated as spirits that are part of this world system. Acknowledged as evil and a real and potent threat, and kick them out as a matter of course! Jesus is who He is and the Holy Spirit is Jesus's Spirit, and the demons have got to go and will go as the onion is peeled.

Here's an essential piece:
To this rapid deliverance practice: removing the demons by their numbers. When the spirits are gathered together under their spokesman, they can be organized for expulsion by requiring the spirit to admit (exactly) how many spirits are under their leadership and authority. If you hear them, fine. If not, ascertain by the Holy Spirit, your intuition or physical response, whether they are legion, many, a few or just a few, for instance.

A Spiritual Warfare Ensemble

Legion - in Jesus`s time a Roman legion was at full strength at 6,658 persons. That's a lot of spirits! Cool, get them all!

Many - hundreds, this is much more common than legion. A real good bag.

A few - dozens, this has a satisfying ring to it. Get them.

Just a few - is self-explanatory. But wait, what, how can there be so many? Well, consider these things are spirits, their corporal selves are often beyond tiny to something larger, or sometimes quite larger, and varying spirit to spirit. But still, mostly little they're just spirits, we are talking about entirely spiritual beings. Usually, it would take very many to make a grain of salt and only a few at a time are coming against us. That is, unless you allow them to run rampant over you, and then all bets are off. To explain, when you attack a larger group of spirits you will be there longer, but not relatively. They are so small, they are wisps of ectoplasm. So going after a bunch is well worth the effort and won't take that much more time and effort in comparison to the haul! So, what are we actually talking about? Here's an example. Its 4:00 a.m., why are you awake? Huh? A spirit manifests, your skin starts crawling and there's a spiritual wet blanket starting at the feet and working its way up! Cool - that's a power spirit! Spirit that is manifesting what is your name? I command you in the name of the Lord Jesus' what is your name? What's your name spirit? There is one here that is greater than you, His name is Jesus! I command you spirit what is your name? "My name is Solata" it finally says. Spirit what is your function. The thing replies "Sleeplessness."

Well, that's appropriate! Solata are you legion? "No." Are you many? "No." Are you a few? "A few, yes." Solata, you've got to go! Now get up, write this stuff down and get after it. Don't worry about your next day and the time right now. Whenever you evict these spirits. You get it done by tying together the spirit with its subordinates, associates, and then all the other spirits contained in "a few." Or "many" and their underlings and associates all-together, (and don't forget the hand motions!). Furthermore, instruct Solata that all commands you give it apply fully to all the spirits that are tied together with it. Isolate it and work your way through the commands from Self deliverance 101 to cut its props out from underneath it, and go! Scoot the things out! Maybe it's been a bad day, and you recognize that spirits have been messing with you, sigh. You're getting harassed, headaches, you're tired, getting thoughts that you don't want and are foreign to a healthy way of thinking. It's not you at all? But you can't shut your mind off! Sigh. Well, here lies your shopping list! All these symptoms can be spirits and they are susceptible to being bundled and cast out! Go for it! It will take you a bit longer to bag the lot, but so what. Especially, when you can find a spirit over "many," perhaps several with "a few." Clearing these spirits out will be well worth the effort. This is where self-deliverance really shines. The kind folks helping you to freedom will work on the spirits the Lord shows them. These will be the spirits that the Holy Spirit knows will win you greater freedom and need to be dealt with, right now, so you can go deeper. You, you're in hot pursuit of all the other spirits! Spirits that would reinforce the ones the Holy Spirit wanted to deal with and would replace them as they fell. Your work is to go after those spirits, the one's rising as you experience greater freedom and try to harm that freedom. You're eviction work will include inactive and dormant spirits that will not have a chance to mess with you in the future, cool! A good catch! Love it. A real demon hostile environment at work! You're a bad house! No demon is too insignificant or too powerful to be skipped over. They have all got to go and now is a good time! And if you do hear them, you don't have to pay any attention to all of that lot! Ignore them.

Better yet, come against them in the "opposite spirit." Again, look for the fruit. Avoid getting severe with them, and cast them out as a matter of course. Avoid at all costs failing to resist them at any opportunity you have. Coming against them in the "opposite spirit" and automatically align yourself with the actual victors - you and the Lord in the power of the Holy Spirit. Glory to God, cool, really excellent! A good day from a bum one! But where do we find the spirits groups we're going after? Physical locations! Biblically, you have three hearts, and here is a good place to begin to clean them out of. You also have a soul, your soul has three components, mind, will and emotions, another fruitful place to explore. Your brain is made up of neurons, synapses and linkages. Your eyes are actually the only part of the brain's style of cells that is outside of the brain's casing. Spirits are looking to hide anywhere you may not think to look! You're something like 60% water, and you have blood coursing all over your body. You possess a skeleton with bones all over the place, glands, organs, tissue and muscles, a blood circulatory system and there you go. It's -imperative that you pray, and ask the Lord to reveal the spirits. Ask him to prompt you to look in all the right places; they can escape us but not the Holy Spirit!

A Spiritual Warfare Ensemble

Functions:
Are what these spirits do, It's not who they are. Eventually, you will throw out all the leadership. Then individual spirits will not have any-one to assign them their tasks, telling them what functions they are to work against you with. They will be uncoordinated, an improved situation for you! They may be "hurtful spirits," imagine all the mischief a hurtful spirit can get involved in! The assignments they'll have can often be a combination of things, varying according to the current leadership's plans in trying to bring you down! And that will change as you toss them out.

A brief listing:
Of possible demon functions: there are false or counterfeit spirits, spirits masquerading as the true Holy Spirit. Jesus and God, false tongues, heart attack spirits, high blood pressure, electrical disturbance of the heart, inflammation is a major one. Man or woman-hating killer spirits. Immediate or slow and agonizing deadly spirits, premature death spirits, spirits that lie in wait until you're elderly! Disease spirits, deception spirits, can be quite powerful! Conflict, anyone heard of any church splits lately? Witchcraft and occult spirits, mediums, the list is huge! That is why you're peeling an onion, and as the onion is peeled different spirits with differing functions arise and try to shuck you into believing you're making too little progress. It's very much a process and really difficult to see the end from the beginning.

Now we'll talk about symptoms:
How are you feeling today? Some feelings and symptoms are natural and may need attended to with the usual medical suspects. Others not so much. For instance, depression, anxiety, oppression, fears of many kinds, confusion, racing mind, destructive thoughts from out of nowhere, conflict and suspicion. Those are demon-driven symptoms. And these are the kinds of symptoms that should interest you, in some ways they are easy to identify; the ones above are pretty simple. The tougher part is finding the spirits behind them. One advantage we have is that as we continue to make progress against our oppressors, some of these symptoms will be automatically dealt with. This is because the spirits driving those symptoms will be thrown out. That's the principal reason that diligence is essential! Keep after them, don't allow them to re-organize against you, get rid of the upper-level spirits as quickly as you can. Seek the Lord, and consider where you are most vulnerable and write that down. Try combining that functional area with getting them out by their numbers so you can rapidly shift the odds in your direction. For instance, what if

you're experiencing shortness of breath, and, well, you're not that out of shape? Go looking for death spirits, heart and circulatory system spirits. Remember to go after the top- level spirits anytime you can find a spirit organization. Concerning heart symptoms go for the strongmen or the spokesman, then cast the spirits out by their numbers. Look into inflammation and heart rhythm affecting spirits, plaque generating spirits, and arterial inflammation spirits. Consult a dictionary or thesaurus - The Demon Hit List - by *John Eckhardt*, is an excellent resource if you're running out of ideas. And this important area needs to be treated as urgent! At first, your job is to get the *top-level spirits* removed as quickly as you can. Then work your way through the functional areas using the numbers approach - for the results for your energy. Lastly, work just with the numbers approach for peeling that onion.

Another absolute essential:
Is to continue working with your deliverers, as they will be hitting areas the demons are trying to keep concealed. And this will yield other areas to explore.

Team work:
Is also an excellent approach; do your best to put this support in place for the sake of your deliverance. Let me emphasize again: that you should use due diligence, and consider possible opposing armies. The demon leadership will bring military-style tactics into play, at any opportunity. That includes building up reserves (organizationally, you can see that as the upper-level spirits personal armoring and reinforcements). And just for a rainy day and you're getting too dangerous, style of reinforcements! Fortunately as the demon leadership stashes these inactive, and dormant spirits away on the lower or lowest levels of the onion, we are ripping and slashing our way down to them. By using our rapid deliverance techniques.

Shutting-the-doors:
An overlooked area, as often the deliverer, is working against the tide, just trying to get as much freedom as available time and energy will allow. The way to shut the doors and gates is to remove the spirits at the *root level!* Utilize the books listed here, for instance, *Prayers that Rout Demons*, by John Eckhardt, has a section dealing with root level spirits, and another for internal gates! This guide and the listed reading materials offer an expansive self-deliverance - Holy Spirit powered - deliverance and sanctification reference. Please exercise discipline and diligence for a thorough purging! This material is meant as a reference and guide only. It assumes the worst- case scenario,

except for those who are cooperating with the demon spirits! Those folks must **stop immediately!** And start actively coming against the spirits in the "opposite spirit," or risk becoming a tool of Satan! And that will not take long! Hopefully, your infestation is minor, but it's impossible to tell exactly as so few folks fully understand what is really going on. Some folks walk away from a partial deliverance and just put up with the misery until they are overwhelmed at a later date. Take this guide very seriously and apply it, and grow as you increasingly batter the gates of the enemy's defenses. This guide has cost me pain, torment and torture in order to learn what was needed for a personal self-defense; please use it! Lastly, at All Nations Church you will find a lending library. It contains some of the following books. **Soul Ties and Legal Ground** - by *Jessica Jones*, **Iniquity** - by *Ana Mendez Ferrell*, **Prayers That Rout Demons** - by *John Eckhardt*, and When **Pigs Move In** - *Don Dickerman*, You could start with "Soul Ties and Legal Ground" and combine what Jones teaches and the lessons from these guides for a really thorough purging; it would be an in-depth "thumb in the eye" against Lucifer's scheme's! Please, get one book at a time, wring every bit of help out of it you can, and do it over and over again as necessary until you run out of any reaction by indwelling spirits! Yes, get scrubbed as clean as a whistle with one any book's help. Then bring it back and get another!

Lord Bless! - Finis…

185

A Word from the Author

A principal reason I did not want to write this book was the possibility of not being believed. It seems that we in this modern, westernized, natural world, where man is the measure of all things. And progressive liberalisms increasingly the rule. Have little to no place for the actuality of all the evil supernaturalism so apparent in our culture, and the church is a part of that very culture. And that is very far from the "Biblical Worldview" of God's Word being the measure, and our obedience a fruit of our faith. But mostly who would I be, to disobey the Lord of my life when the Holy Spirit dropped this task on me. On reflecting on the world of Christ Jesus where the occult was the worldwide standard and the demonic was the enemy, which He came to defeat, everywhere. For all eternity for all the willing. And legally observant but spiritually recalcitrant religion, was the closest organized thing to God in all the globe. And His enemy. It seems the Bible remains entirely the truth today as then, and we shouldn't cherry pick it. And the supernatural is as much a part of the landscape today as it was then, everywhere, when you don't cherry pick it. So I am glad now that I wrote it and expect you'll find real value here. I was told that I write as I speak, and that might challenge the grammarians.

Sorry, but this is my best effort and my prized project, and I have come to realize that indeed it does read better spoken aloud, particularly the second book its dynamite when read aloud! It's also an odd subject, being quite mad yet perfectly sane; it's tough to portray. Perhaps these scribbling's can lead to some further insights on the subject of the schizophrenic and the demonized people amongst us, particularly the Christians. They can be successfully helped, should they choose, should they be afflicted as I was to some degree. And that is if they've been made aware of the efficacy of all this! But mostly I remain grateful to have reached full deliverance from the demonic, not so many do. But not to worry, most people will hear the things that so assault them in deliverance sessions and those that do not, can still be helped. The Holy Spirit is the spirit of Jesus, and He has all authority on heaven and earth and delegates it to us, for this purpose amongst others. The manner of my deliverance has led me to explore and explain some other rather unusual, yet wholly biblical concepts perhaps not so popular just now. But I surmise that is changing, it seems we are in the last of the last days, and the demonic is really ramping up. As Lucifer desperately tries to stop the work of the future history of the church triumphant crashing down on his rotten head. Yes, it's personal to me; they're real, Lucifer, the satanic and the whole despicable assembly.

Even so, come Lord Come.